New Zealand Travel Guide: Typical Costs, Weather & Climate, Visas & Immigration, How To Pack, Food, Hiking, Cycling, Top Things To See And Do And The Best Sights

by Alex Pitt

Contents

Introduction

New Zealand is the adventure capital of the world. Hiking, skydiving, caving, bungy jumping, skiing — everything here is geared towards getting you outside and doing something incredible. As a popular destination for backpackers and budget travelers, New Zealand is really affordable and offers many ways to save money. I loved my time in New Zealand — the people were friendly, the country was beautiful (I can see why the shot Lord of the Rings there), and you meet a lot of great travelers there. It's one of the best countries in the world and a place not to be missed. I've never heard anyone not love their time in the country. Most people don't want to leave! I didn't. You really can't go wrong with this majestic country. It's one of my top ten countries in the world! Use this guide to plan the adventure of the lifetime on a budget!

As the planet heats up environmentally and politically, it's good to know that New Zealand exists. This uncrowded, green, peaceful and accepting country is the ultimate escape.

Walk on the wild side

There are just 4.6 million New Zealanders, scattered across 268,021 sq km: bigger than the UK with one-fourteenth the population. Filling in the gaps are the sublime forests, mountains, lakes, beaches and fiords that have made NZ one of the best hiking (locals call it 'tramping') destinations on earth. Tackle one of nine epic 'Great Walks' – you've probably heard of the Heaphy and Milford Tracks – or just spend a few hours wandering along a beach, paddling a canoe or mountain biking through some easily accessible wilderness.

The Real 'Big Easy'

Forget New Orleans… NZ can rightly claim the 'Big Easy' crown for the sheer ease of travel here. This isn't a place where you encounter many on-the-road frustrations: buses and trains run on time; roads are in good nick; ATMs proliferate; pickpockets, scam merchants and bedbug-ridden hostels are few and far between; and the food is unlikely to send you running for the nearest public toilets (usually clean and stocked with the requisite paper). And there are no snakes, and only one poisonous spider – the rare katipo, sightings of which are considered lucky. This decent nation is a place where you can relax and enjoy (rather than endure) your holiday.

Māori Culture

If you're even remotely interested in rugby, you'll have heard of NZ's all-conquering All Blacks, who would never have become back-to-back world champions without their unstoppable Māori players. But this is just one example of how Māori culture impresses itself on contemporary Kiwi life: across NZ you can hear Māori language, watch Māori TV, see main-street marae (meeting houses), join in a hangi (Māori feast) or catch a cultural performance with traditional Māori song, dance and usually a blood-curdling haka (war dance). You might draw the line at contemplating ta moko, traditional Māori tattooing (often applied to the face).

Food, Wine & Beer

Kiwi food was once a bland echo of a boiled British Sunday roast – but these days NZ chefs find inspiration in new-world culinary oceans, especially the South Pacific with its abundant seafood and encircling cuisines. And don't go home without seeking out some local faves: paua (abalone), kina (sea urchin) and kumara (sweet potato). For picnic fodder, head to NZ's fab farmers markets. Thirsty? NZ's cool-climate wineries have been filling trophy cabinets for decades (sublime pinot noir and sauvignon blanc), and the country's craft-beer scene is exploding. Contemporary coffee culture is also firmly entrenched.

Typical Costs and Money

Accommodation – Hostel dorms cost between 20-40 NZD per night, while private rooms begin at 80 NZD. Free Wifi is not offered at every hostel, so if you require an internet connection be sure to double check your booking. Very few hostels include free breakfast, and only some hostels offer self-catering facilities. Budget hotels begin around 70 NZD per night for a double room. Free WiFi is common, though very few hotels include free breakfast. Airbnb is widely available with shared accommodation starting around 27 NZD per night and entire homes starting at 70 NZD per night. There are also a ton of campgrounds throughout the country with rates around 15 NZD per night. Couchsurfing is huge here too.

Food – Eating out is generally expensive here. A restaurant meal with a drink with table service can cost about 35-40 NZD per person. Of course, you can find cheaper meals if you stick to Chinese, Korean, and Japanese restaurants (sushi is actually quite cheap). They cost around 10 – 15 NZD. You can find sandwiches for 8 NZD and fast food like McDonald's or Burger King will cost between 7-15 NZD. A beer at the bar will cost around 8 NZD. If you choose to cook your food, plan to spend between 65-80 NZD per week for basic food stuffs.

Transportation – Getting around the country is fairly cheap. Local bus fares vary for each city, but prices are generally around 3 NZD for an adult (less if you purchase metrocards). The intercity bus system is quite inexpensive and the Naked Bus (it's just a name!) has promotional fares for 1 NZD if you book far in advance. Otherwise, most fares are about 20 NZD, though slightly more if you are going long distances. For example, the long Auckland to Wellington trip will cost around 40 NZD. Bike rentals are available in most cities, with daily rentals costing around 15 NZD per person (which generally includes a helmet and lock). Flying can be expensive since there isn't a lot of competition among airlines here. Book 2-3 months in advance for the best flight deals. There are also backpacker hop on/hop off buses. They are expensive and cost between 200 – 800 NZD but include a lot of activities and are a fun way to meet other people.

Activities – Activities run the gambit and can cost between 100-600 NZD. There are a lot of outdoor activities and tourism here is constructed around getting people outside. Budget extra for activities as they will be your biggest expense while you are here. For more specific price information, visit the city-specific guides.

Suggested daily budget – $70-90 NZD / $50-62 USD (Note: This is a suggested budget assuming you're staying in a hostel, eating out a little, cooking most of your meals, limiting your adventure activities, and using local transportation. Using the budget tips below, you can always lower this number. Remember, if you stay in fancier accommodation or eat out more often, expect this to be higher!)

Money saving tips

Free WiFi – The internet on New Zealand is slow and expensive (though it is getting better!). McDonalds and libraries offer free wi-fi but don't expect many places to offer free internet.

Learn to cook – Since eating out is expensive, the best way to save money is to cook your own food. While the cafes in New Zealand are good, you don't miss out on first-rate cuisine by cooking your own meals. When it comes to buying groceries, the cheaper supermarkets are Pakn'Save or Countdown.

Choose wisely – Tours cost a lot of money in New Zealand. A few of these are enough to bust any budget and send you home before you had planned. Pick the ones you really want to do and save the rest for another trip.

Hit happy hour – The backpacker bars have cheap happy hours offering 5 NZD drinks. Hit them up and drink for cheap. Otherwise, plan to spend around 8 NZD for a beer at the bar.

WWOOF it – WWOOFing is a great way to work for your accommodation and food. In return for working on a farm or B&B, you get free food and board. It's a popular activity with travelers because it lets you stay in a place cheaper and longer. You can do it for a few days or a few months. Keep in mind, most farms will require you to have some experience, as too many inexperienced workers have caused trouble in the past.

Clean in exchange for your room – Many hostels let you trade a few hours of cleaning and making beds for free accommodation. Ask when you check in if this is possible — it might just save you some money!

Car share – Car shares are a popular transportation option for travelers looking to lower costs — all you need to do is chip in for gas. You can find rides on websites like Gumtree, Craigslist, or Jayride. Additionally, you'll see people asking for rides on hostel bulletin boards.

Couchsurf – While there are not a ton of options available in the country, there are hosts in all of the major cities. If you don't mind sleeping on a couch or floor, this is a great way to save some money and meet locals (and get a free place to stay).

Hitchhike – Hitchhiking is common throughout the country and generally safe to do. It's quite popular with backpackers so if you aren't interesting in doing a rideshare, this is another option. Just use your head before getting into a car!

Take a free walking tour – There are a few free walking tours in New Zealand, like Auckland Free Walking Tour in Auckland or WellyWalks Limited in Wellington, that offer visitors (and locals!) insight into each city. If you want to get beneath the surface of New Zealand then this is a great place to start.

Tipping and service charges

Tipping in New Zealand is not obligatory, even in restaurants and bars. However, tipping for good service or kindness is at the discretion of the visitor. Hotels and restaurants in New Zealand do not add service charges to their bills.

Banking

New Zealand banks are open from 9.30am to 4.30pm Monday to Friday. Some are also during weekends. Automated Teller Machines (ATM's) are widely available at banks, along main shopping streets and in malls. International credit cards and ATM cards will work as long as they have a four-digit PIN encoded. Check with your bank before leaving home.

Bringing cash into New Zealand

There is no restriction on the amount of foreign currency that can be brought in or taken out of New Zealand. However, every person who carries more than NZ$10,000 in cash in or out of New Zealand is required to complete a Border Cash Report.

Currency exchange

Foreign currency can easily be exchanged at banks, some hotels and Bureau de Change kiosks, which are found at international airports and most city centres.

Currency values

Coins have values of 10, 20 and 50 cents, $1 and $2.

Notes have values of $5, $10, $20, $50 and $100.

Goods and services tax

All goods and services are subject to a 15 percent Goods and Services Tax (GST) included in the displayed price. Visitors cannot claim this tax back, however when a supplier ships a major purchase to a visitor's home address the GST will not be charged.

Swedish rounding

Due to the discontinuation of 1c, 2c and 5c pieces, purchases made in New Zealand are subject to "rounding" of amounts either up or down. The Reserve Bank believes most retailers are adopting the Swedish Rounding System. Under this system prices, ending in 1 to 4 cents will be rounded down and prices ending in 6 to 9 cents will be rounded up. For example, a purchase of $15.14 would be rounded down to $15.10, and a purchase of $15.16 would be rounded up to $15.20. It is at the retailer's discretion how they handle prices ending in 5 cents.

Top things to see and do in New Zealand

Stay awhile in Queenstown – The action capital of the country, this is one of the most fun cities I've ever visited. There's a lot of outdoor activities and sports (bungee jumping is the most popular) to do in the area, amazing restaurants, and the best nightlife in New Zealand. Everyone who comes ends up staying longer than planned. Don't skip Fergburger either — they have the best burgers in the country!

Get your LOTR fix at Tongariro Alpine Crossing – Labeled the best one-day hike in New Zealand, this walk takes you through where they filmed Mordor in Lord of the Rings. You walk through volcanic terrain, near high peaks, and sulfur lakes before finishing off in a dense forest. The walk takes a full day and is actually quite challenging. Your legs will probably be sore for a few days afterward but it will be worth the sense of accomplishment that comes with completing the hike. Expect to pay around 50 NZD per person.

Relax in the Bay of Islands – North of Auckland, this area has some of the best opportunities for dolphin and whale watching, relaxing on the beach, swimming, boating, and eating seafood. The area is very low key and is a popular summer and weekend getaway destination for Aucklanders. A bus from Auckland to Paihia will cost around 20 NZD.

Bungy jump – Any adrenaline seeker worth their salt will do the 500 foot Nevis Bungy Jump outside of Queenstown. If that's too high, there are smaller ones in Auckland and Queenstown. The price of adventure isn't cheap, however, with a single jump at Nevis costing 250 NZD.

Skydive – Another popular adventure activity in New Zealand is skydiving. The best place for this is over Lake Taupo. It provides a stunning backdrop as you plunge to Earth from 15,000ft. A jump from 12,000ft will cost you around 300 NZD, while a jump from 15,000ft that includes a video, photos, and t-shirt is 550 NZD.

Visit Abel Tasman National Park – Located in the south island, this national park looks like something out of Asia with its turquoise blue water, dense jungles, and warm temperatures. There are many multi-day hiking trails and beautiful sea kayaking throughout the park. Entry to the park is free, though you will need to pay 14 NZD for a campsite if you plan on staying over. Huts are also available for 32 NZD per night.

Hang out in Wellington – New Zealand's capital has great architecture, character, fantastic nightlife, restaurants, and cultural activities. I found it to be the most "artsy" city in New Zealand. There's a lot of cultural activities to do here so don't be like other travelers and rush through — it's worth a few days!

Experience the Waitomo Glowworm Caves – Explore these caves in sheer darkness with nothing but the glow of glowworms to guide your way. It's an exciting activity as you float down rivers and jump over waterfalls and watch the "starry sky" in the cave. You can also tube and rappel through the caves too. It was one of the highlights of my time in the country. Prices will vary depending on what activities you do in the cave and expect to pay at least 150 NZD for the activities.

Watch a Maori cultural show – Maori culture is important to understanding life in this country. You find Maori symbols and words throughout the country. See a cultural show while you are there to get a better understanding of the life and history of the country's native population (the most popular ones are in Rotorua). Evening shows that also include dinner cost around 120 NZD per person.

Go dolphin and whale watching – Whether you go from the Bay of Islands, Auckland, or down in the south island, the country is the migratory route for many of these creatures and you're bound to see lots of them no matter when you go. Expect to pay between 60-150 NZD per person.

Go skiing – During the winter months, the south island, especially the are around Queenstown, has snow covered mountains that offer some of the best skiing in the southern hemisphere. Prices will vary depending on where you go, how you get there, what equipment you rent, and how long you go for, but expect to pay a few hundred dollars per person.

Unwind in Rotorua – Rotorua is famous for its Maori cultural shows and for its sulfur smell. All around the city are sulfur mud pits that give the city a unique odor. But the upside is that there are a tone of thermal spas in the area to relax in!

Get outdoors in Kaikoura – This is a coastal town several miles north of Christchurch. It is set in a peninsula, which makes it an awesome place to enjoy the mountain scenery while watching for whales or dolphins. Additionally, there are is an interesting museum, a handful of historical sights, and the Maori Leap limestone cave.

Wander through Wellington Botanic Gardens – Of all the beautiful gardens throughout the country, this is perhaps the most popular. There is a vast tract of native forest, in addition to an international plant collection, a rose garden, and a landscaped area — complete with duck pond, playground, sculptures, a café, and more. Entry is free.

Ride the gondola – If you are in Christchurch, the gondola ride is highly recommended and a pretty fundamental experience. The ride starts on the Heathcote Valley floor and takes you up the side of Mount Vaendish. There is a nice restaurant at the top that allows you to peer out over the landscape as you eat. Many people cycle or walk back down. Adult tickets are 28 NZD, while children pay only 12 NZD.

Weather, climate & seasons

From the crisp days of spring to the burnt orange beauty of autumn, New Zealand is a traveler's paradise.

New Zealand's climate is mild, and ranges from subtropical in the north to temperate in the south. No matter the season, the majority of our main attractions are open year-round.

Spring: September - November

During spring, New Zealand bursts with new life. Colourful blooms, baby wildlife and 'waterfall season' makes this an inspiring time of year to visit.

Temperatures range from 4.5 - 18 degrees celsius (40 - 65F).

Temperature & weather

Average daytime temperatures during spring range between 19 degrees Celsius (66F) in the north to 16 degrees Celsius (60F) in the south. Expect a mixture of weather – crisp, sunny days can briskly change to cooler temperatures with spring showers.

Spring's blooming outdoors

Spring is our 'waterfall season' – the country's falls multiply with magnificent effect. It's the most impressive time of year to take a tour to Milford Sound via the Milford Road.

The fruit-growing areas of South Island's Central Otago are bedecked with blossom. Alexandra's annual Blossom Festival is held each year when the town's cherry trees are in full bloom.

Explore Auckland's Waitakere Ranges on foot – tiny fern fronds dot the lush native bush during this time of year.

Spring is a great time of year to visit the Hobbiton Film Set; the charming bluebells and Middle-earth gardens are in full flower. See glorious 360-degree images of Hobbiton here.

Explore world-class vineyards in Hawke's Bay as well as their prestigious Food and Wine festival, FAWC, or explore the great outdoors on one of New Zealand's Great Walks or Cycle Trails.

Travel tips for Spring

Booking in advance

During September and October, booking in advance isn't always necessary. If you are planning to travel during November, popular accommodation and activities can start to be booked up, so reserving early is recommended.

Our highways are open year-round

New Zealand's highway network is nearly always open, especially during Spring. Some roads in the south of the South Island, including the Milford Road, can sometimes be affected or closed by adverse weather.

Springtime Skiing

Depending on snowfall, New Zealand's ski resorts usually close in late September. The best time for skiing is late June, July and August.

Summer: December - February

New Zealand's many beaches and lakes are perfect to cool off during the summer months. Summer activities tend to make the most of the sun, sea and sand.

Temperatures range from 21 - 32 degrees celsius (70 - 90F).

During summer, New Zealand celebrates. The majority of kiwis take their annual break over the Christmas period and flock to scenic beaches or lakes. Discover our top picks for the ultimate summer vacation in New Zealand.

Temperature & weather

With average high temperatures ranging from 21 degrees Celsius to 25 degrees Celsius (77F), summer in New Zealand is hot without being muggy. Sunshine hours are high, and rain is not overly common in most places.

All things sun, sea & sand

Being an island nation, you're never far from the sea in New Zealand. Make the most of long, hot summer days with beach picnics, kayaking, snorkeling, sailing or swimming – the list is endless!

During this time of year our native Pohutukawa tree blooms a vibrant red, justifying its name as New Zealand's 'Christmas Tree'.

Swim with dolphins, walk coastal trails and feast on delicious seafood – for kiwis, summer is all about indulgence and celebrations.

It's a great time of year to learn to surf. Places like Raglan, Taranaki and Mount Maunganui are surfing meccas.

Rotorua's world-famous mountain biking trails, dotted with enormous Redwood Trees, are dappled with shade – the perfect way to stay cool!

Heli hiking on ancient Franz Josef Glacier is a great activity for the hotter months, when there are clear skies and little rain.

Stroll the quaint French-colonial streets of Akaroa, the site of New Zealand's first and only French colony.

Travel tips for summer

Make reservations in advance

Being high season, booking in advance for accommodation, tours and transport is highly recommended.

Take a tour

Be prepared for busy roads – taking a tour is a great option to allow you to sit back and soak up the sights.

Don't forget the sunscreen

New Zealand's sun can be harsher than in other parts of the world. If you're outside exploring, wearing sunscreen with a high SPF is highly recommended to avoid sunburn.

Autumn/ Fall: March - May

In autumn, New Zealand enjoys some of the most settled weather of the whole year. Soak up long, sunny days and golden leaves with hiking, cycling or kayaking.

Temperatures range from 7 - 21 degrees celsius (45 - 70F).

Discover the places and experiences that come alive during March, April and May.

Temperature & weather

Long, sunny days tend to linger long into New Zealand's autumn, and with average high temperatures of between 18C and 25C, you'll hardly notice summer has 'officially' ended. Nights begin to get chilly around mid-April. Because it's no longer high season, you won't encounter the busy crowds of summer.

Colourful landscapes and settled days

One of the most special things about Autumn in New Zealand is the colors – especially in the Hawke's Bay and Central Otago regions. Deciduous trees turn brilliant hues of yellow, gold and hot orange, and it's all set against a sky that seems far too blue to be true.

Long, still days lend themselves to the great outdoors – Autumn is the perfect time of year to hike one of our nine Great Walks, explore a cycle trail or try fly fishing.

During March and April it's still hot enough to swim in most places. Cool down with a dip in the ocean after exploring the coastline.

Celebrate the creative quirkiness of the kiwi culture at the Hokitika Wildfoods Festival, where delicious local delicacies like huhu grubs and whitebait patties are cooked up by colorful locals.

Salt water fishing is exceptional from March to May. Take a local charter boat or dangle a line off the coast.

Orca and dolphins visit Wellington's coast during the Autumn months. Watch from the city's waterfront or catch a ferry to Eastbourne or Picton.

Travel tips for autumn

Where to see Autumn/Fall color

New Zealand foliage is evergreen, but exotic species are common throughout the country. The most impressive places to see the burnt oranges, yellows and reds of autumn (fall) are Central Otago and the Hawke's Bay, but botanic gardens throughout the country promise to put on a show.

Scenic alpine passes

From late April, high mountain passes can be subject to snow and ice, so taking a tour is a good option. If you would prefer to self-drive, carrying chains is recommended.

Winter: June - August

The winter months brings snow blanketing soaring mountains in certain parts of the country and clear, crisp days that awaken the senses. Hit the ski slopes, visit a winery or two or head along to one of the many winter festivals.

Temperatures range from 1.5 - 15.5 degrees celsius (35 - 60F).

Temperature & weather

While our winter months do bring cooler weather and rain to parts of the country, many locations only experience a mild winter. High temperatures range from between 10 to 16 degrees Celsius (50 – 61F), but our 'winterless North' hardly experiences colder days at all. In the South Island, frosts and heavy snowfall is common – ski season is world-class.

Crisp sunshine and snowy mountains

The ski fields are in full swing, and the mountains of the Central Plateau, Canterbury and Central Otago are blanketed with fresh snow. Snow enthusiasts should make a point of trying several different ski fields a go – in Queenstown and Wanaka, there are four world-class ski fields within an hour and a half of each other. For a thrill, try heli-skiing, snowboarding, cross country skiing or sledging.

In Auckland, temperatures are mild and sunny days are common. It's the perfect time of year to hike up Rangitoto – chances are you'll have the dormant volcano all to yourself.

New Zealand is home to some impressive, naturally heated hot pools. There's nothing like soaking weary bodies at the end of a long day skiing or exploring.

Winter is a great time to explore the historic gold mining and Kauri logging towns of the Coromandel – you'll feel like you've stepped back in time.

In the Hawke's Bay, the cooler months are a time for delicious citrus fruits and hearty vegetables. Head to the Havelock North farmer's market to make the most of locally grown, fresh produce.

Between June and July the Matariki festival is held throughout New Zealand. Matariki has always been an important time in the Maori calendar – strongly connected to the seasons, Matariki is a celebration of the upcoming year.

Travel tips for winter

New Zealand is a year-round travel destination

Most attractions, activities and locations are open all year in New Zealand, and if you're travelling during the cooler months, you don't need to book ahead. Some water sports may not be on the agenda because of cooler temperatures, and the official Great Walks season doesn't run during winter – you can still hike many of the tracks if you are experienced, but huts won't be serviced.

What time of year can I see the All Blacks play?

The winter months are your best bet to see the All Blacks play a home game, but booking in advance is highly recommended because tickets are always very popular.

The best time for skiing

A world-class ski destination, New Zealand's ski fields will be covered in a thick blanket of powdery snow from June to September. Head to Ruapehu, Canterbury, Queenstown or Lake Wanaka for thrilling snow sport action, but be sure to book accommodation, ski passes and gear hire in advance.

Visas & immigration

Visitors are welcome to New Zealand. So to ensure you have an experience to remember, it's a good idea to make sure you've done your homework and have everything sorted before you leave.

When you arrive, you'll need to ensure your passport is valid for at least three months beyond your intended departure date, and if required, have a valid New Zealand visa.

Holidaying in New Zealand

You do not need a visa to visit New Zealand if you are:

- A New Zealand or Australian citizen or resident,
- A UK citizen and/or passport holder (you can stay up to six months), or
- A citizen of a country which has a visa waiver agreement with New Zealand (you can stay up to three months).

If you don't meet the above, then you'll need a visitor visa, which allows you to holiday in New Zealand for up to nine months. If you're applying as an individual, the easiest and cheapest way to apply for a visitor visa is online. If you're travelling with a partner, family or group, you should submit a paper application.

Working holidays

Working holiday visas are available to young people, usually aged 18-30 (but 18-35 in a select few countries). They let you travel and work in New Zealand for up to 12 months, or 23 months if you're from the UK. To apply you'll need to meet the visa requirements, and have:

- A return ticket, or enough money to pay for one; and
- Be coming mainly to holiday, with work being a secondary intention.

Work visas and staying permanently

If you're thinking of coming to New Zealand to work for a few years, or maybe even to settle, you'll need a work or resident visa. To get that – you're likely to need a job. For information about working in New Zealand, including industry profiles, tips on job hunting, and a list of job sites to check out, visit New Zealand Now.

Transiting through New Zealand or Australia

If you are travelling to New Zealand via an Australian airport, you may also need an Australian visa – consult your travel agent or airline if you are unsure. Transit visas will also be needed for all people travelling via New Zealand, unless they are specifically exempted by immigration policy.

More information about visas

On arrival

You will need to complete a Passenger Arrival Card before passing through Customs Passport Control. A passenger arrival card will be given to you during your flight. If not, cards are available in the arrival area.

What you can bring into New Zealand

After you've cleared passport control, you should collect your baggage and proceed through customs and biosecurity checks. In order to protect New Zealand and its environment, certain items are not allowed to be brought into the country, have restrictions for entry or must be declared if they are deemed to present a biosecurity risk. These include food, plants, animal products and outdoor recreational equipment.

Your baggage may be sniffed by a detector dog and/or x-rayed, and it may be searched to identify any risk goods you might be carrying.

To avoid penalties it is best to familiarise yourself with these guidelines prior to travel. For a detailed list of prohibited, restricted or declarable items, please visit Ministry for Primary Industries (biosecurity agency).

Allowances and duty free concessions

As a visitor to New Zealand you may be entitled to various concessions and duty free entries on some of your goods. If you are 17 years or older, you are entitled to allowances for alcohol, cigarettes and tobacco.

Transport around New Zealand

Driving

Self-drive is a popular way to explore New Zealand. Before renting a car or campervan, make sure you're familiar with driving in New Zealand.

Driving in New Zealand is different to driving in other countries. What do you need to know before getting behind the wheel?

Exploring New Zealand's beautiful landscapes by car, campervan or motorhome is a popular way to get around. Even if you're used to driving in other places, you need to be well aware of things like weather extremes, narrow, windy roads and different road rules before you begin on your journey.

What's different about driving in New Zealand?

We drive on the left hand side of the road and our vehicles seat the driver on the right.

Always drive on the left hand side of the road in New Zealand. If you're used to driving on the right hand side of the road, this can be a challenge to remember especially when pulling out into traffic. Remember - if you are driving, you must be seated in the middle of the road – your front seat passenger will be the on edge of the road.

Never drive when you are tired and take regular breaks.

It doesn't matter what country you are driving in, it is extremely dangerous to drive when you are tired. Visitors to New Zealand might be tired because of jet-lag, early starts and late nights, or because they had a long day driving the day before. Because driving in New Zealand can be very different to other countries, you need to be well-rested and alert – tired drivers are dangerous drivers.

Many roads have varying conditions, and can be narrow, windy and cover hilly terrain.

New Zealand's diverse terrain means roads are often narrow, hilly and windy with plenty of sharp corners. Outside of the main cities, there are very few motorways. Most of our roads are single lane in each direction without barriers in between. You may also encounter gravel roads. It's important to allow plenty of time, go slow and pull over in a safe place if traffic wants to pass from behind you. Take plenty of breaks so that you stay alert.

It's easy to underestimate drive times when looking at a map.

Maps don't show how narrow and windy roads can be. What might look like a short trip can take a long time. For example: Hokitika to the town of Haast, a popular drive for visitors stopping to see New Zealand's glaciers, is 278km (172mi) on the map and may look like a short 3-hour drive. However, drivers should allow for up to 4 hours' of driving time because of the windy road. This is common all over New Zealand – always allow for more time than you think you'll need.

Weather-related hazards are commonplace.

In New Zealand, you might experience four seasons in one day. It's possible to start your day off with blue sky and sunshine, but arrive at your destination in rain and hail. Because of this, weather related hazards on the road can occur at any time. Always check the weather forecast before departing, and adjust your plans accordingly. If you're driving in the South Island in winter, spring or late autumn, snow is a possibility – ensure that you're carrying chains if a cold snap has been forecast. Most rental companies will provide you with chains and demonstrate how to fit them. Read our winter driving tips.

Winter roads can be treacherous.

Snow, ice and fog can be common in winter, especially in the South Island and around mountain passes. Ensure you're clued up on the weather forecast for the region that you're driving in, leave large following distances and make sure you're travelling with snow chains (and know how to fit them).

Not all New Zealand rail crossings have automatic alarms.

Only half of the 1500 rail crossings in New Zealand have automatic alarms. When red lights are flashing it means a train is coming so stop and only proceed once the lights have stopped flashing. Other crossings have a 'Railway Crossing' sign and give way or stop signs only. If you see this, stop, look both ways and only cross the track if there are no trains approaching.

In addition to the above, it's a good idea to get familiar with important New Zealand road rules before your arrival.

Public transport

New Zealand's public transport includes buses, trains and ferries. Find out how to get around without hiring a vehicle.

Buses are the main form of public transport in New Zealand, with some areas also offering trains, ferries and trams.

Public transport between cities

Bus

Buses are the cheapest and most common form of public transport available for travelling between towns and cities. Intercity and Naked Bus are the two main providers of this service, and fares start from around NZ$10.

Although not public transport, hop-on hop-off buses are also a popular way to get around New Zealand, especially among backpackers. Choose your pass and make up your itinerary as you go along.

Train

Trains are not a common form of public transport in New Zealand; however there are three main train lines operated by KiwiRail: Auckland to Wellington (Northern Explorer), Picton to Christchurch (Coastal Pacific), and Christchurch to the West Coast (the TranzAlpine - considered one fo the most scenic rail journeys in the world). Train tickets start from around NZ$49 per person.

Ferry

Ferries are popular for travel between the North and South Islands. The two major providers are InterIslander and Bluebridge, and fares start at NZ$55 for foot passengers. Taking the ferry means you'll experience the beautiful Marlborough Sounds on your way into or out of Picton.

Ferry travel is also available between the mainland and New Zealand's offshore islands, including Waiheke, Rangitoto and Great Barrier near Auckland city, and Stewart Island just below the South Island. In some coastal areas, ferries connect towns which are closer via water than via road – including Russell and Paihia in the Bay of Islands.

Water taxis are smaller vessels which offer a scheduled service visiting the small ports which ferries can't reach – handy for reaching out of the way hiking and mountain biking spots in places like Queen Charlotte Sounds and Abel Tasman National Park.

Domestic flights

Flights are easy to catch from city to city, and no flight is longer than two hours.

Flights in New Zealand are both easy to organise and very affordable, making air transport a popular choice for travel around the country.

You can fly between all New Zealand cities and most major towns using domestic air services. Air New Zealand and Jetstar are the main providers. Their services are complemented by regional airlines, charter companies and scenic flight operators.

Tours

If you'd like a pre-planned itinerary and someone to drive you, your local travel agent can help you find the perfect tour.

Travel Agents, Agencies and Airlines

The travel agents listed here can help you plan and book your trip to New Zealand, whether you're on a budget or wish to experience a luxury holiday.

If you see a '100% Pure New Zealand Specialist' logo beside a travel agent listing, it means they are an accredited expert on New Zealand airlines, accommodation, activities, and more. They have undertaken specific training with Tourism New Zealand to increase their knowledge of our country.

While you're there

i-SITE Visitor Information Centres

i-SITE information centres can help you plan and book activities, accommodation and transport once you're here in New Zealand.

i-SITE knows all the best things to do, places to stay and ways to get there. Plus they'll take care of the bookings.

Every person who works at i-SITE is a travel expert for their own home town, so they can help you to find the sort of activities, attractions, accommodation and transport that only a local would know.

You can be sure that once you have experienced the latest and greatest of what one place has to offer, i-SITE will help connect you with their equally friendly i-SITE colleagues at the next stop on your journey.

So whether you've come around the world or down the road you can rely on i-SITE for expert local knowledge and bookings throughout New Zealand.

Itinerary planning and information

Bookings nationwide - accommodation, transport, activities, attractions

Free maps, weather & mountain safety information

Local information - events, attractions, restaurants & more!

Internet, phone and electricity

Find out how to stay connected to the internet and phone services during your trip.

Chances are that you're arriving in New Zealand with a mobile phone, tablet or laptop – or a mixture of all three. If you're looking to stay connected to the internet and phone services everywhere you go, it's recommended that you purchase a plan from one of New Zealand's main networks. Note that mobile coverage is not available in some rural and wilderness areas.

Free WiFi hotspots are generally found in main cities only and can be sporadic throughout the rest of the country. Purchasing a plan from a network will allow you to have access to a mix of data, calling and texting throughout your trip to suit your communication and connection needs.

Mobile networks in New Zealand

The main networks are:

- Vodafone
- 2degrees
- Spark
- Skinny

You'll need to take your mobile device(s) into a branch when you first arrive to purchase your pack. Use the branch locator to find the most convenient location for you.

If you're looking to use a combination of devices to connect to the internet, it is most cost-effective to set up your phone as a wireless hotspot that your other devices can run off as well. You can purchase data packs that expire after a certain amount of time. The network you choose will advise you on what will work best for your needs.

If you choose to purchase a mobile data pack with Spark, you'll be eligible to access their free WiFi hotspots, dotted throughout the country. Find out more about where these hot spots are here.

Data/mobile costs

Data and mobile packs range from $19, depending on how much data you require and how long you are in New Zealand.

Free WiFi

New Zealand currently has limited access to free WiFi services, although the situation is gradually improving. Free WiFi hotspots are found predominantly in urban areas and are not common in small towns or rural regions.

All of New Zealand's Public Libraries have a free WiFi service. Find a library near you.

Many i-SITE Visitor Information Centres provide free WiFi service. Download a map of all i-SITEs with WiFi access.

Some cafes and restaurants also have a free WiFi service when you purchase food or drink.

Prepaid mobile packs from Spark include 1GB of free WiFi data per day at more than 1000 hot spots throughout New Zealand.

Free WiFi in city centres

Free WiFi service is available in central Auckland, Rotorua, Wellington and Dunedin.

Free WiFi and accommodation

Some of New Zealand's accommodation providers provide free WiFi for guests. It's a good idea to check if this service is offered at the time of booking.

Public Phones

All public phones take call cards purchased from bookstores and newsagents. These require you to call a free 0800 number, enter the pin code from the card, and then make your call. Some public phones also accept credit cards, but very few accept coins.

New Zealand phone numbers can be found online in the White Pages (alphabetical listings, including business and residential) and Yellow Pages (business category listings).

Electricity

New Zealand's electricity supply runs at 230/240 volts, and uses angled two or three pin plugs (the same as Australia and parts of Asia).

Most hotels and motels provide 110 volt ac sockets (rated at 20 watts) for electric razors only. For all other equipment, an adapter/converter is necessary, unless the item has a multi-voltage option.

Health and safety

New Zealand is generally a very safe place to travel with a relatively low crime rate, few endemic diseases and a great healthcare system.

Visitors are still advised to take the same care with your personal safety and your possessions as you would in any other country, or at home. Take copies of your important documents (like your passport and credit cards), and keep them separate from the originals. You should also keep a record of the description and serial number of valuable items (like cameras, tablets and smart phones). And remember, in an emergency dial 111.

Keeping yourself safe

Carry a mobile phone and don't hesitate to dial New Zealand's emergency phone number if you feel unsafe or threatened - dial 111. Calls are free.

Travel with someone you know and trust whenever possible.

Don't accept rides from strangers and don't hitchhike.

If you're out at night, keep to well lit places where other people are present. Don't take short cuts through parks or alleyways. Take a taxi or get a ride with someone you know.

Avoid accepting drinks from strangers and never leave your drink unattended.

Carry a basic first-aid kit for use in emergencies.

Keeping your possessions safe

Always lock your accommodation and vehicle and keep windows secure when you're not around.

Store valuables securely, ideally in a safe at your accommodation. Never leave valuables or important documents in parked vehicles.

Never leave bags, backpacks, wallets or cameras unattended in any public place, especially airports, ferry terminals or bus/railway stations.

Don't carry large amounts of cash or expensive jewellery.

If withdrawing money from a machine, withdraw small amounts only - preferably during the day - and shield your pin.

Don't leave maps, luggage or visitor brochures visible in your vehicle. These are obvious signs that you are a tourist and may have valuables.

If you are travelling by campervan, park it in designated areas whenever possible.

If any of your possessions are stolen or valuable items misplaced, advise local police as soon as possible.

Staying safe in New Zealand's natural environment

Most visitors come to New Zealand to enjoy our unique natural environment but visitors can underestimate the risks associated with the great outdoors.

A walk in a city park is very different to a walk in a National Park. Take the time to learn about where you are going and to seek advice from others, especially your local i-SITE or Department of Conservation (DOC) Visitor Centre on how to be best prepared.

1. Cell phone coverage: Coverage is unreliable outside of the main city centres and if you are venturing into the bush or the mountains you are unlikely to get reception Consider carrying a personal locator beacon and a battery powered radio, especially if you're travelling alone.

2. Changeable weather: New Zealand's weather can change extremely quickly and can be severe at times. A day that starts out sunny may turn cold, wet and windy. You must always be prepared for wet, cold weather if you are heading out into the bush, the mountains or onto the water. On days when it is sunny, remember that New Zealand's clear, unpolluted atmosphere and relatively low latitudes produce sunlight stronger than much of Europe or North America, so be prepared to wear hats and sun block. Always check the weather forecast and be prepared for four seasons in one day. Check weather conditions and any alerts by DOC before you set out on a walk or hike. Treat all weather warnings seriously.

3. Challenging terrain: Don't underestimate any "walk" outside of the main centres. You need to be reasonably fit to enjoy our bush, mountains and national parks. Check out the recommended level of fitness required for any walk before you head off. You also need the right clothing and proper footwear. A cheap raincoat will not keep you warm and dry in the bush or in windy conditions. Shoes that you wear on the street will not be good enough when you are walking on muddy tracks or climbing over rocks.

4. Tell someone where you are going: Tell someone your plans and leave a date for when to raise the alarm if you haven't returned. Leave a detailed trip plan with the Department of Conservation

(DOC) or a friend including a "panic" date, the more details we have about your intentions, the quicker you'll be rescued if something goes wrong. You can find a handy Outdoor Intentions form on the AdventureSmart website.

5. Be prepared for anything and everything: Being well prepared means considering everything above. You need the right clothing, footwear and equipment, and make sure you have enough food and water to cover you in an emergency. Follow all safety precautions as per the outdoor safety tips on the AdventureSmart website.

6. If lost, seek shelter and stay where you are. Use a torch/camera flash to attract attention at night. Try and position something highly coloured and visible from the air to help a helicopter search during the day.

Safety in the water

New Zealand's extensive coastline and network of waterways provide ample opportunity for swimming, boating and fishing. However many people are unprepared for the potential dangers of the water.

I recommend that you visit Water Safety or AdventureSmart for advice on how to stay safe on New Zealand's beaches and waterways.

If in doubt, stay out.

Never swim or surf alone, or when cold or tired.

Swim between the flags. Beaches with potential hazards are often patrolled by lifeguards, who put up yellow and red flags. Between these flags is the safest place to swim. Listen to advice from life guards.

If you have children with you, watch over them at all times.

Learn to recognise ocean rip currents.

How to get help?

The emergency telephone number in New Zealand is 111. It is a free phone call.

If you have an emergency and need a quick response from the Police, the Fire Service, Ambulance or Search and Rescue, dial 111.

There are Police Stations in all main towns and cities in New Zealand and in many rural locations. Contact details can be found in local telephone books.

Don't hesitate to contact the police if you feel unsafe or threatened. Report any theft and crime to the police immediately.

Keeping safe via text messaging

Vodafone, Telecom and 2degrees offer a txt messaging service for visitors.

You can send updates about your location and travel movements via txt to number 7233 [SAFE]. These details are kept on a central database which can be accessed by police if necessary.

Each text message sent to 7233 will be acknowledged by an automated response, which advises you to call 111 and request police assistance if you are in danger.

Police and the New Zealand tourism industry encourage you to use this service as another way of letting people know where you are and what you are doing while in our country.

Accidents and health insurance

With a little care and common sense, your visit to New Zealand should be accident free. If you are injured here, you may need the help of the

Accident Compensation Corporation (ACC) - New Zealand's accident compensation scheme.

In New Zealand, you cannot sue anyone for compensatory damages if you are injured. Instead ACC helps pay for your care - and that means paying towards the cost of your treatment and helping in your recovery while you remain in New Zealand.

You still need to purchase your own travel and medical insurance because ACC does not cover everything:

ACC only covers treatment and rehabilitation in New Zealand, and usually you must pay part of the cost yourself.

ACC does not pay any additional costs resulting from an accident, for example delayed or curtailed travel costs, travel home, treatment at home and loss of income in your home country.

I strongly advise you to arrange your own health insurance. New Zealand's public and private medical/hospital facilities provide a high standard of treatment and service, but it is important to note these services are not free to visitors, except as a result of an accident.

Medication and vaccinations

Visitors bringing in a quantity of medication are advised to carry a doctor's certificate to avoid possible problems with New Zealand Customs. Doctor's prescriptions are needed to obtain certain drugs in New Zealand.

No vaccinations are required to enter New Zealand.

How to pack for a New Zealand adventure

There are few places on Earth as diverse as New Zealand, both in its landscapes and in the possibilities of what to do in those landscapes. It's quite feasible to be kayaking in translucent ocean one day, standing atop alpine summits the next, and bouncing on the end of a bungee cord somewhere in between.

The abundance of adventures produces another challenge in itself – what to pack? Each different activity demands some tweaking of gear, so here's a guide to the essentials of kitting yourself out for that next Kiwi adventure.

On the trail

Weather moves fast and often furiously across narrow New Zealand, making layering the key to comfort. A base layer of a Merino or polypropylene thermal top (and maybe bottoms if you're heading to alpine country) is the foundation, and there should be a mid-layer, preferably a fleece or softshell jacket. The outer layer needs to be a breathable and waterproof rain jacket.

New Zealand tramping tends to err on the mountainous side, be it among the snow-tipped Southern Alps or the volcanoes of Tongariro National Park, which generally means cold nights, so prepare ahead by packing a down jacket, gloves and a warm hat. For many walkers, hiking shoes have usurped boots, but the predominance of mountain hikes in New Zealand means that the country contains some of the most rugged hiking terrain in the world. Across scree and boulders, boots will be preferable. If you plan to stick to coastal walks such as the Abel Tasman Coast Track or Cape Brett Track, good-quality hiking shoes should suffice.

Tramping's great essential is a backpack. If you're planning to stay in huts, of which there are almost 1000 in New Zealand, a 50L to 60L pack should be large enough, but if you're going to be camping, you'll probably need to stretch to a 70L or larger pack. For day walks, a 22L to 35L daypack should be sufficient. Be sure to add some waterproofing to the pack – many come with built-in rain covers, but otherwise the best bet is to line the pack with a dry bag, which can come in sizes up to 90L.

On popular tramps, such as the Milford and Routeburn Tracks, huts typically contain gas cookers, eliminating the need to carry a stove, but on other overnight hikes you may need a stove and cooking pots. The Department of Conservation website lists every hut and its facilities, so check ahead.

Snow cover

When winter powders New Zealand's mountains, hiking boots get replaced by ski boots. The basic principles for packing to stay warm in the snow are the same as those for hiking – get layered. Wear Merino or polypro thermals against the skin then a fleece or softshell jacket as your mid-layer. The most essential item of all is a windproof and waterproof outer layer – ideally a good ski jacket and ski pants – because nothing will dampen a good day on the slopes quite like, well, getting damp.

The cold tends to hit your extremities first – feet, hands, head – so invest in quality thick socks, insulated gloves and a warm hat. Wearing a pair of thin liner gloves under your snow gloves provides an extra layer of warmth. Pocket hand warmers, which you simply flex to create heat, are another good option for an instant shot of heat to keep fingers and hands mobile. A buff will provide warmth around the neck.

Snow goggles or sunglasses are a must in the snow, and if you plan to spend hours out on the slopes, carry a small day pack – 20L to 30L – in which you can pack away layers as needed and carry snacks and sunscreen.

Re(cycled) gear

New Zealand is a cycling dream, with a network of 22 routes known as the New Zealand Cycle Trail now stretching for 2500km across the country. Most of the routes can have you in the saddle for a few days, making comfort paramount.

A pair of cycling knicks (padded shorts) are a must if you want to be thinking about scenery more than saddle soreness. If you're going to be spending time sightseeing as well as cycling during the day – or just feel coy about the Lycra look – a good compromise is a pair of 'shy shorts', or double shorts, which look like an ordinary pair of shorts but have a padded pair of knicks attached inside.

A pair of padded cycling gloves will ease the burden on your hands (and protect them from the sun), and the potential of cold New Zealand mornings – especially if you're cycling on the South Island – make cycling arm and leg warmers a good investment. These can easily be pulled on and off as the day and your body warms or cools.

Cycling shirts should be made of breathable, wicking material that dries quickly. Sitting on a bike for hours can expose you to plenty of sun, so consider packing a few long-sleeved shirts as protection for your arms while cycling.

Heavy-duty hiking-style rain jackets are likely to feel bulky and restrictive on a bike, so carry a lightweight rain jacket that's also breathable, or even a softshell jacket that combines warmth and wind-stopping qualities with water resistance. In a region like the West Coast, however, the potential for solid downpours makes a dedicated rain jacket a necessity.

Paddle packing

How you pack for a kayak trip will largely depend on where you're paddling – kayaking around icebergs in Tasman Lake is a very different beast to paddling in the bright, sunlit ocean of Abel Tasman National

Park, but water and the expectation of getting wet is the common denominator.

Quick-drying shorts and shirts will provide the most comfort, while the lack of sun protection on the water makes a wide-brimmed hat and long sleeves the smartest approach. Cycling or kayaking gloves can negate the prospect of blisters. Wet feet are inevitable as you climb in and out of the kayak. Wetsuit booties make for excellent kayaking footwear, but equally good (and more versatile) are outdoors sandals, which dry quickly and double as land shoes in camp or if you're combining the kayaking with a bit of walking.

One with the lot

If you're coming to New Zealand with a varied list of adventures in mind, versatility is key in your suitcase. Pack so that you can layer in any circumstance – a night in the mountains, a day on water, a morning on the ski slopes. Merino thermals are the Swiss army knife of dressing for the outdoors, providing multiple options, while you should bring a breathable waterproof and windproof rain jacket that'll cope with the worst conditions – it's better to be overprotected than underprotected against the conditions in New Zealand's wilderness.

Versatile hiking shoes might be preferable over purposeful hiking boots if tramping is just one component of your plans, and quick-drying shorts and shirts will be your best friend on all of your adventures. Trousers with legs that zip off, converting them to shorts, can be good when you're packing with multiple active possibilities in mind.

Don't overlook Auckland, embrace it

Can you think of another city built on dormant volcanoes, with pristine beaches close to the city centre and neighbourhoods rich with restaurants and art? New Zealand's biggest city, Auckland is more than a stopover city for the Pacific, it offers travellers the perfect intersection of urbanity and geographical beauty.

Most travellers will fly into Auckland – sometimes mistaken for New Zealand's capital but that mantle belongs to Wellington – before heading off to explore Lord of the Rings country at Matamata, or the volcanic terrain of Tongariro National Park. You should book in time to uncover the harbour-side city's diverse offerings as well.

Encompassed by ocean scenes and sounds

Coined the 'City of Sails', Auckland floats on two glistening harbours, Waitemata and Manukau, both of which are gloriously speckled with large ferries, luxury yachts and comparatively humble boats that voyage to nearby islands and waterside towns. Sensational beaches are within reach of cosmopolitan Auckland via Highway 1.

Don't miss the Whangaparaoa Peninsula, about a 25-minute drive from Auckland's city centre, for waves that crash onto flawless white sand shores, such as those at Orewa or Red Beach.

On the same coast is Shakespear Regional Park (not Shakespeare), perhaps one of the only places on the earth where one can waltz through dense rainforest one minute, and gallop through colossal paddocks that overlook the ocean the next. Yes it's an odd intersection of landscapes, but an exciting one.

In the Hauraki Gulf, Waiheke Island is a reason to visit Auckland in itself, reached via ferries running from the city. Among the islands' many draws is its wineries found in the depths of regional hills. Visit some of the country's most renowned producers, including Te Whau, Stonyridge and Obsidian, and taste their produce with a sparkling ocean backdrop.

Adventure is still on hand

In Māori, Auckland is referred to as 'Tāmaki Makaurau', meaning 'an isthmus of one thousand lovers'. Auckland is actually a narrow straight with about 50 volcanoes – all inactive – giving way to opportunities for hikes and mountain biking close to the city centre.

Queenstown might be the 'adventure capital', but extreme activities are easily found in Auckland too. The city's alternative to bungee jumping: the 192-metre sky jump at Auckland's Sky Tower does a feet first dive, instead of heads.

Next, try rainforest canyoning in the hidden pools and gorges of the Waitakere Ranges is ideal for those who seek a stepping stone before bungee jumping or skydiving.

For travellers with a need for speed, there are jet boat tours that whiz through the city's waters; one of the quickest and most exhilarating ways to get to know the harbour.

With more time on your hands, I recommend slowing things down and exploring the harbour on a kayak instead. I challenge travellers to find a city where it's possible to depart the city centre, head to a volcanic island, let's say Rangitoto for Auckland's sake, climb to the top and watch the sun sensationally disappear over the city skyline before paddling back.

Culinary and artistic gems

New Zealand's food scene is in the midst of an awakening, and with some of the best produce in the world at its fingertips it's no surprise Auckland plays host to myriad of top-notch restaurants. The city is also favoured with a rich history of immigration, creating an amalgam of restaurant offerings to rival cities like New York, Melbourne and London.

This is best personified by Britomart. Once the mercantile mecca of colonial Auckland, Britomart has been rejuvenated into a shopping and dining precinct, through a series of cobbled walkways.

Italian is best at Ortolana, a garden-to-table glasshouse bistro serving up meticulously composed pasta and salad dishes, each featuring only three or four main ingredients, treated with utmost respect and care.

For Italian with a view however, head to Amano on the water, a multifaceted eatery set in a building more than a century old, where a modern industrial fit-out sets the tone. Amano is a bakery, cafe and restaurant all at once, serving house-made pasta and pairing it with some of New Zealand's best seafood – including Wairarapa Coast crayfish and Auckland Island scampi.

For travellers lucky enough to find their Auckland stay coinciding with the weekend, a morning can be wisely spent visiting the La Cigale French market. Bubbling pans of paella, crepes, and waffles fill stalls and stomachs, while the trade of fresh breads, pastries, cured meats and cheese takes place to the beat of live music.

Auckland also has an abundance of Asian eateries on its side – Japanese, Chinese and Indian restaurants are plentiful: see how the Kiwis represent food from the region. One of the city's most celebrated contemporary Indian restaurants is Cassia, which fuses classic ingredients and present-day techniques to form dishes such as tandoori fish with smoked yogurt, macadamia, and sorrel.

When the dining has passed and it's time for a drink, the setting of Auckland's summer twilight is hard to beat, where institutions such as Devonport's Devon on the Wharf provide cocktails graced with mesmeric views of the harbour.

Need to walk all that tasty food off? There is no better city to be in. Auckland's small land mass makes it easy to navigate by default. Its humble and petite nature fortuitously gives way to a tight congregation of streets painted with culture...literally! K Road's inspiring street art precinct in Newton houses enthralling building murals covering all styles and subjects, from bohemian to political.

K Road is an interesting contrast to Auckland Art Gallery, only a 20-minute walk away in upmarket Parnell. No bigger collection of Māori treasures and artworks is found anywhere else in the world. This public gallery continues to showcase the greatest parts of historical and present-day New Zealand – a condensed version of what Auckland seems to encapsulate as a whole.

A typical weekend... usually involves trawling one of the city's farmers markets like the one at La Cigale in Parnell, or heading out of town to take in the surf beaches, forest walks and vineyards of west Auckland.

While I'm out west, I'll often stop in for craft beer and a leisurely lunch at Hallertau's beer garden in Riverhead. They usually have good live music on Sunday afternoons too. If I'm out west from November to January, I'll detour to Muriwai Beach to check out the newly-hatched fledglings at the Takapu Gannet Refuge.

To soak up some history and culture...I always recommend that visitors to the city spend time at the Auckland Museum. The museum's Pacific Island and Māori collections are especially interesting for travellers from the northern hemisphere, and it's always worth checking out what special exhibitions are on. Recently I've taken in great one-off displays on Kiwi pop and rock music and the history of Air New Zealand. Major international touring exhibitions are often installed at the neoclassical building, which is located in Auckland's wonderfully vast, 80-hectare leafy Domain.

Auckland's one of the most culturally diverse cities on the planet...with almost 40% of the population born overseas. One benefit of this blend of cultures I particularly enjoy is the best eating in New Zealand. For regional Chinese cuisine I like the Balmoral area around Dominion Rd, especially the hand-pulled noodles at Shaolin Kung Fu, and from there's it's just a short hop to the Indian spice shops and Sri Lankan restaurants around Sandringham. My go-to spot for cheap eats is 7 Siri Taste of Sri Lanka.

It's a great city if you're feeling festive...as there are plenty of special events to take in over the year. During the last weekend of January, the city's anniversary commemorations include the annual Anniversary Day Regatta when the harbor is packed with colourful yachts. My favourite festivals are Pasifika celebrating Auckland as the biggest Polynesian city in the world, and the Auckland International Cultural Festival, both in March. You'll usually find me there watching Somalia play Iraq in the soccer mini-World Cup, while I'm combining Ethiopian curry and injera flatbread or snacking on Chilean empanadas.

When I'm celebrating something special...it's always a toss-up between one of Auckland's more established eateries like The French Cafe or Merediths, and trying one of the newer places that always seem to be popping up in areas like Grey Lynn, Mt Eden and Kingsland. I'll usually begin with drinks at a bar like Golden Dawn or Freida Margolis before dining on modern Thai at Saan or Japanese-Peruvian cuisine at Azabu. The Ponsonby Central precinct is always a fail-safe place for a special night out too.

New Zealanders love their sport...and I'm no exception. From March through to October the NZ Warriors (rugby league) and the Auckland Blues (rugby union) are the main teams to watch, and if I'm not in the grandstand at Mt Smart Stadium or Eden Park, you might find me enjoying the game over a few Kiwi brews at Galbraith's Alehouse. I'm pretty excited New Zealand has won back the Americas' Cup in yachting because having the next regatta in Auckland will improve exciting waterfront developments like Wynyard Quarter and Viaduct Harbor even more.

Summer in the city... is a great time to experience all the goings-on around Silo Park at the harbor front Wynyard Quarter area. I'm a big fan of the outdoor weekend movie season down there, with flicks ranging from Monty Python's Life of Brian to Kiwi classics like Goodbye Pork Pie. The films usually kick off at 9.00pm, but it's wise to get there earlier to secure a good spot and enjoy the food trucks, free live music and DJs.

The best views in town...are atop Auckland's volcanic craters – don't worry, they're all dormant or extinct! I'm fond of taking a walk up Mt Eden or One Tree Hill for panoramas over the two natural harbors that the city has been built around. I've also negotiated the 192m-high SkyWalk on top of Auckland's Sky Tower, base jumped down, and lived to tell the tale!

A good spot to stay… for travelers include Ponsonby, Mt Eden and Devonport. They're all linked to the city and ferry terminals by decent

48

public transport, so it's easy to get out to the islands of the Hauraki Gulf. All three suburbs have chilled neighborhoods and a selection of great bars and restaurants.

When I want to get out of the city...my friends and I jump on a ferry and zip across to Waiheke Island. There's plenty to do throughout the year, and it's definitely worth spending at least one night staying over there. Standout places for a leisurely winery lunch include Poderi Crisci or the Shed at Te Motu. And yes, the unsealed road out to remote Man O'War Bay is winding and a bit bumpy, but where else can you taste superb chardonnay and swim just meters away at a sublime beach?

The ultimate guide to planning a Queenstown ski trip

During New Zealand's winter months' skiers and snowboarders from all over the world descend upon picturesque Queenstown to explore its surrounding ski fields. But with four winter resorts to choose from, how do you decide where to ride? Here's everything you need to know before you go.

Which resort?

All four snow resorts – each with its own ski school and on-mountain restaurants – are suitable for beginners through to experts, but of course everyone has their favorite. About 15km (25 minutes' drive) from the center, Coronet Peak is the closest resort to Queenstown and therefore the busiest. With a good combination of wide open pistes and well-groomed trails, there's plenty of fun to be had here. It might be Queenstown's lowest resort, but a multimillion-dollar snowmaking system ensures good cover throughout the season.

On a clear day, you can see The Remarkables (also known as 'Remarks') ski area, 24km (37 minutes' drive) from Queenstown, across the valley from Coronet Peak. The two resorts are linked, allowing you to save a few bucks by purchasing a multi-day pass that can be used at either resort; hand it in at the end of your trip to recoup your NZ$5 deposit. Despite having 220ha of skiable terrain to Coronet Peak's 280ha, The Remarkables is higher and thus receives more powder days. It also has an excellent terrain park, and offers some amazing off-piste for expert riders when there's adequate cover.

An hour's drive from Queenstown (43km), Cardrona is particularly popular with families for its wide open basins, abundance of intermediate terrain, and excellent childcare facilities. With world-class freestyle facilities including two halfpipes, it's also a hit with snowboarders.

Another half an hour's drive north of Cardrona (27km past Wanaka), Treble Cone requires the furthest trek for fresh lines, though you'll thank yourself for making the effort. Linked to Cardrona, with similar discounts for multi-day ski pass purchases, Treble Cone is the highest and largest ski area on New Zealand's South Island, and also boasts the longest vertical (700m) of Queenstown's winter resorts. With plenty of challenging off-piste to explore, Treble Cone is most popular with advanced riders, but there's also a special slope for beginners, and several long, leg-burning intermediate runs. Cashed-up powder hounds may also be interested in heli-skiing options in the area, or cat-skiing at the private Soho Basin resort near Cardrona.

Self-drive or ski bus?

A handful of ski bus companies offer daily return services to all four resorts from a range of departure points (around NZ$30-55 per person return); stop in at Queenstown's Visitor Information Centre (22 Shotover St) for more info. By opting for one of these services, you won't have to worry about fitting snow chains to your rental vehicle (never fun!) or stress about having to navigate the region's mountain roads, which can get a little hairy.

Alternately, self-driving affords the flexibility to make last-minute decisions about where to ski each day, and leave a resort whenever you wish. With multiple car rental outfits located at Queenstown Airport, it's super easy to arrange car hire, and if you're in a group of more than two, self-driving is likely to be more cost-effective. All ski resorts have free parking.

Where to go for après ski

With more than 40 drinking dens packed into one square kilometer, the sheer volume of Queenstown bars makes up for the lack of ski-in access. Options run the gamut from kitsch to classy; alpine-themed Rhino's Ski Shack and the new incarnation of local institution World Bar are just two great starting points. For cocktails, head to Little Blackwood, The Bunker, or Bardeaux, which has a particularly extensive wine list. If it's a dance-on-tables sort of night, boogie down to Winnies on The Mall.

Still in your ski boots? Stop in at the historic Cardrona Hotel for a mulled wine on your way back to Queenstown from Cardrona or Treble Cone.

Where to soak it up

For a small town, Queenstown has a surprisingly varied dining scene spanning Mexican to mod-NZ flavors. Don't leave town without sampling a 'fergburger' from the eponymous burger bar, which are totally worth the hype (and the queue). Next door, Fergbaker is a top spot to grab a coffee and a pastry before jumping on the ski bus of a morning. If you'd prefer to sit down (and keep drinking), Pub on the Wharf has an excellent NZ$20 dinner menu, as does nearby Atlas Beer Café.

For those after something a little more high-end, head to Madam Woo for fancy Malay-Chinese street food, or indulge in some seriously fine NZ dining at Rata, helmed by Michelin-starred chef Josh Emett. If you're planning to take a day off skiing, schedule a lazy brunch at hip

Bespoke Kitchen, which offers one of Queenstown's best breakfast menus.

Beyond skiing

Whether you're looking to take a break from the slopes or don't ski at all, you'll be pleased to know that most of Queenstown's top activities are available year-round. For adrenalin junkies, there's skydiving, jet boating, paragliding, quad biking and whitewater rafting. You can also brave one of several canyon swings and bungee jumps including the Nevis Bungy – at 134m it is New Zealand's highest.

Slightly less extreme pursuits span horse riding to snowshoeing, to taking the Skyline Gondola to Bob's Peak above Queenstown for activities including Ziptrek (a zip lining ecotour) and the gravity-fed Skyline Luge, while more relaxing options include wine tours, brewery tours, Lake Wakitipu's Underwater Observatory, lake cruises, Lord of the Rings tours, or simply soaking away your cares at the plush Onsen Hot Pools overlooking Shotover Canyon.

Make it happen

Hugging a pretty inlet on Lake Wakatipu with sweeping views of snow-capped mountains beyond, Queenstown is a stunner year-round. Just 6km from town, Queenstown Airport is serviced by regular buses and taxis, and while you will need to book ahead for accommodation during ski season (late June to early October), there is no lack of options at all price points in and around town. And Queenstown's compact center brims with restaurants, bars, ski gear and rental stores, and is easily navigable on foot.

For those looking to ski solely at Treble Cone or Cardrona, consider picking up a hire car from Queenstown airport and bedding down in more low-key yet equally scenic Wanaka, 67km northeast of Queenstown.

Kiwi secrets: New Zealand experiences you've never heard of

It may be synonymous with adventure sports, epic scenery from The Lord of the Rings films and the spine-tingling haka of the All Blacks rugby team, but New Zealand has plenty of unique but lesser-known experiences for travelers. That isn't so surprising, really – this far-flung country adrift in the South Pacific has a long history of invention and innovation.

Admire flappers in Napier and steampunks in Oamaru

Art deco fans with eyes on Miami and Mumbai's architectural heritage should also set their sights on Napier on New Zealand's North Island.

Rebuilt in the 1930s after a devastating 7.8 magnitude earthquake, the city center bursts with pastel colors, graceful buildings and geometric designs. In February each year, usually around Valentine's Day, Napier townsfolk pull out the stops for a weekend-long celebration of all things '30s – vintage cars, flapper fashions, speakeasies and brass bands. Any other time of the year, stop by the Art Deco Centre on the beachfront and book a walking tour to appreciate the detail you would otherwise overlook.

On the South Island, the once-neglected seaside town of Oamaru remained relatively unchanged after its 19th-century economic heyday, leaving most of its Victorian buildings intact. Over the last decade or so, an influx of creatives and bohemians has transformed the town into the 'steampunk capital of the world'. Steampunk, which grew from a sci-fi subgenre to encompass fashion, film and other arts, reimagines modern technology against the backdrop of a steam-powered Victorian England. Begin your exploration of this fascinating subculture at the Steampunk HQ, a gallery in the 1830s-era Meeks Grain Elevator Building. The town's Victorian Precinct is also home to antiquarian bookshops, vintage stores and artisan shops.

Climb a ladder like no other in Wanaka

Queenstown, the winter sports capital of New Zealand, is a must-visit destination year-round, but nearby Wanaka should be on your itinerary too. Among its many worthwhile sights is New Zealand's only via ferrata. Wildwire Wanaka is a relatively new set-up in the foothills on the way to Tititea/Mt Aspiring National Park where even the most danger-adverse of travelers can stretch themselves by 'basically climbing a ladder' as the owners put it; it's no ordinary ladder, however – this one ascends past the spectacular Twin Falls, offering epic views as part of a wow-did-I-really-do-that adventure. Wildwire run half- and full-day excursions, depending on your level of fitness (and tolerance of vertigo).

Test your nerves on a sky walk in Auckland

Even if your visit to New Zealand is so brief you don't get out of Auckland, you can still have a Kiwi adrenaline experience to tell the grandchildren about. The tallest building in the Southern Hemisphere – the 328m-high Sky Tower – is located in downtown. At its 192m mark sits an observation floor where the gutsy can step past the glass and 'sky walk' around a narrow metal gangplank. There are safety harnesses, of course, but there is no handrail to grip while your legs turn to jelly, making this experience all the more extreme. If the height makes your head spin, concentrate on the 360-degree views of the harbor (and not the city below!). Still not satisfied? You can also bungee-jump off the building...

Aurora hunting and stargazing in the South Island

The aurora borealis (Northern Lights) gets much more attention, but did you know that there is an equivalent light show in the Southern Hemisphere: the aurora australis (Southern Lights)? This celestial phenomenon can be seen from the bottom of New Zealand's South Island, particularly between March and September. Head down to The Catlins, Invercargill and Lake Tekapo, plus Dunedin if you're lucky, to witness the spectacle. You'll need to find a rural location away from light pollution on a dark, moonless night to increase your chances. For night-sky gazers that get all this way but miss out on the aurora, Lake Tekapo is one of the world's International Dark Sky Reserves and New Zealand's best spot for some serious galaxy searching. Nightly tours head up to the observatory on Mt John for spectacular Milky Way views from the University of Canterbury's telescopes.

Helicopter to the volcanic White Island

Not a budget experience but one you'll never forget: imagine hopping aboard a helicopter in renowned Rotorua (bucket list material already, with its geothermal activity and Māori culture) then flying to New

Zealand's only permanently active volcano to explore on foot. Located just off the east coast of New Zealand's North Island, visitors to White Island can wander the crater floor and see sulphur formations, steaming vents and hot streams up close. The island is privately owned, making the whole experience feel as if you might stumble across a Bond villain's lair while you're there. The aerial views of the volcano, and Rotorua's lakes district, are all thrown in for nothing.

Get muddy at Mudtopia in Rotorua

Your childish, not-yet-satisfied desire to get covered from head to toe in thick brown muck can finally be fulfilled if you're in Rotorua in December. Mudtopia is a three-day music and mud festival held at this center of outdoor activity on the North Island. For wellness devotees, there is a spa with mud massages, mud facials and mud beauty treatments (Rotorua's mud is packed with restorative minerals). For everyone else, there are pools of mud to slosh around in, mud games, a mud run and a muddy obstacle course – describe by the organizers as 'a kids' bouncy castle on steroids, covered in slippery mud'.

Sashimi your own rainbow trout at Lake Taupo

The unbelievably clear and surprisingly warm waters of Lake Taupo, bordered by the snow-crested peaks of Tongariro National Park, are a magnet for nature lovers who walk, cycle, or canoe the lake. It's also a haven for trout fishing with most anglers plucking out a fish or two. Even if fishing is not your thing, someone is going to land one in these well-stocked waters, so why not try your knife skills and sashimi it on the boat for lunch instead? After your unbeatably fresh meal, take a dip in the pristine lake, then take an excursion to see the Mine Bay Māori rock carvings.

A museum for motor heads and fashionistas at Invercargill

Where would you go to see the largest private truck and car museum in the world? Italy? The USA? Try Invercargill, New Zealand's the most southerly city. In a 15,000-sq meter chamber you'll find Bill Richardson Transport World, filled with restored vehicles that range from the Ford Model T to VW Kombis and everything in between. In a typically Kiwi kook these machines are complemented with exhibitions of New Zealand-created Wearable Art. If you're visiting in June, you can book tickets to the Wearable Art gala, a spectacle of color and creativity. Bill Richardson does not leave the motorcycle enthusiast wanting either. In 2016 the museum purchased a collection of 300 restored and unrestored beasts made from 1902 onwards, and moved them from Nelson to a new museum, the Classic Motorcycle Mecca, in Invercargill's city center.

New Zealand's North Island: on the road at the edge of the world

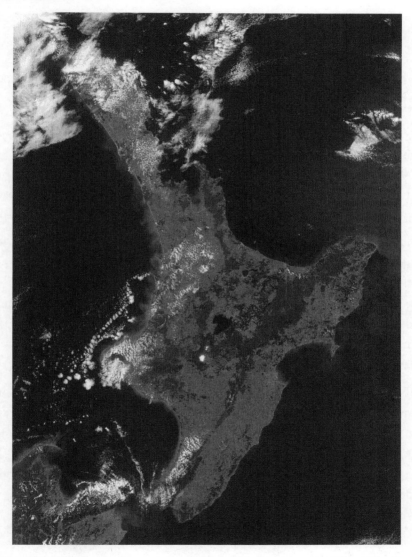

The Māori call them mākutu, or witchcraft, because in New Zealand the roads are magical. One minute they surface, unfolding along pastoral foothills; the next they vanish, furrowing deep into Triassic-period jungles laden with silver ferns. It is an untamed corner of the universe that rewards those travelling under their own steam.

With the keys to a campervan, drivers can – on a whim – go in search of a lake glimpsed through the window, or stop to climb a hill spotted in the rear-view mirror – because their bed for the night is never somewhere distantly ahead, but always about two feet behind them.

Catch the wild waves at Piha

Setting out on the highway from Auckland to the west coast town of Piha, the Kiwi enchantment begins to take hold. Anyone driving to the surfer's retreat must first negotiate the Waitakere Ranges, an abrupt vegetative Eden of subtropical kauri forest that acts as a barrier between the twinkling lights of civilization and the untamed coast.

After a 30-minute drive west, the road corkscrews into hills carpeted with nīkau palms, some as giant as pantomime beanstalks, then careers down the other side to meet Piha's sheer cliffs, pock-marked with nesting sites for gulls. It's mid-afternoon when the campervan trundles into Piha, passing scattered weatherboard houses and parking in front of a beach being pounded by waves. This volcanic sand has Marvel-superhero strength, so rich in iron it will stick to a magnet.

New Zealand's surfers are also drawn here, and talk about it in poetic terms matched only by the place's name itself – Piha is the Māori word for the onomatopoeic crack of surf sliced by the bow of a canoe. The town is so laid-back and low-key that if the surf club were to shut, it'd surely disappear off the map completely. Following a different clock to the rest of New Zealand, surfers rise with the tides and the streets empty at sunset.

With his sun-bleached mop of tousled hair, national longboard champion Zen Wallis embodies Piha's surfing ideal. He's out on the water most days, catching break after break as they blow in off the Tasman Sea,

60

before darkness finally sends him ashore. (He even admits to sleeping with his board before a competition, for luck.)

Also a surf coach, Zen has a deep knowledge of Piha and talks about its waves in reverential metaphors. The predominant onshore wind, he explains, creates a potent hit, attracting only hardened surf-addicts to the town. 'Life existed in black and white before the sport arrived here,' he says, the sky turning oily purple behind him. 'Now we wake every day to a kaleidoscopic, world-class wave, but without the crowds. It's like a drug.'

See glowworms at Waitomo Caves

The campervan rolls south out of Piha in the haze of early morning. Grey banks of cloud shift across the glossy hills and fields where gangly sheep farmers round up super-sized flocks numbering more than a thousand.

Neither the livestock nor the terrain at the western edge of the North Island would look out of place in the Welsh valleys. Evergreen vales and dimpled pastures surround the one-street town of Waitomo, while, beyond the roadside, rumpled farmlands and wool sheds are a picture of serenity. Flocks doze on mossy crags as local farmers watch a rugby game in town. Calm, peaceful and seemingly unremarkable, this place gives nothing away of the preternatural treasures hidden below the topsoil.

Even in a country as geographically blessed as New Zealand, the Waitomo Caves command a special status. A network of fathomless, pitch-black passages, they are places long sacred to the Māori, but also to speleologists like Angus Stubbs, a third-generation farmer-turned-caver. For the past 20 years, this modern-day caveman has found sanctuary in their honeycombed caverns and sunken potholes. They are the North Island's cathedrals, he says, created by millennia of water erosion and now home to a subterranean river and labyrinthine tunnels.

The local Kawhia tribe used the area's limestone catacombs as burial sites to access the afterlife, but the Victorians were more interested in what they could take away. They plundered the caves one by one, digging up museum-piece curiosities and the skeletons of giant moa birds. A flightless creature hunted to extinction by the Māori, its bones fetched a fine price at auction back in London.

Angus leads the way down into the Ruakuri Cave, the midday sun vanishing behind the snap of a trapdoor. Squeezing through narrow gaps into a cavernous obsidian-black hangar, our eyes adjust to the darkness. And then they appear: thousands of underground stars lighting up the vaulted gallery like a lattice of subterranean sky.

'These little fellas are just like me,' says Angus, shining a torch on the glowworms, known first to the Māori as 'titiwai' – water stars. 'Not pretty when the lights are on, but beautiful when it's dark.'

Chill out at Lake Taupo

To drive the North Island is to encounter signposts that tell the story of New Zealand, a curious mix of towns named by homesick Scots and Englishmen – Hamilton, Hastings, Cambridge, New Plymouth – and sing-song Māori villages: Matamata, Whatawhata, Mangatangi.

From Waitomo Caves, the road to Lake Taupo turns southeast onto State Highway 30. It rolls over concertina-creased hills and livestock grids into the North Island's agricultural heartland, dewy and green with vegetation. Soon overtaken by volcanic ridges and treeless mountaintops, the road emerges at Lake Taupo, one of the grandest waterbodies in the southern hemisphere.

Filling the caldera of a prehistoric volcano, the lake was created by one of the largest eruptions in history – one that blew out so much detritus that it would have made Krakatoa look trifling. When Taupo first appears over the dashboard, it looks more sea than lake. It's a body so big that the water and sky mix like a watercolor; one so wide that the Earth curves across its surface like a spoon.

Outside Taupo, on the town's northern outskirts, is the workshop of Delani Brown, a master carver who crafts allegorical totems inspired by the lake and by the Māori creation myth of Ranginui, the sky father, and Papatūānuku, the earth mother.

'The wood can take me in any direction,' he says, tightening a lumpen block of petrified swamp kauri in a vice. 'So I have to listen to it carefully.' As the afternoon passes, the slab gradually undergoes a metamorphosis into an intricate talisman. Delani uses his chisel like a fine paintbrush, delicately etching marks and paring back the block one shave at a time. Up close, it has whittled tattoo lines across its brow; each groove simulates the area's synergy of rivers, canyons and fault-lines.

Proud of his accomplishment, Delani looks out towards Lake Taupo. 'Ko wai koe?' he asks me. 'Which waters do you come from?' It is a traditional greeting born from whakapapa, the fundamental principle of genealogy that permeates all Māori culture. He hesitates for a moment before pointing to the lake. 'That's my universe,' he says. 'Right there.'

It's not just Māori like Delani who have been bewitched by the Great Lake Taupo region. Ever since the first tribes arrived in the 13th century by canoe, the low-slung villages dotted along the lake have attracted newcomers. These days, the acacia-banked edges are filled with the guesthouses, galleries, organic wineries and craft breweries that keep holidaymakers here for days. Many will make the trip out by boat to the high bluffs at Mine Bay, to bob in front of a magnificent stone-faced god carved into the cliffside.

Before dark, the campervan is back on the road and the next 30 miles' zip by with the tempo of a radio pop song. We veer south to the lakeshore town of Turangi, parking by the waterside and lighting a brazier under a half-moon sky. Dinner is lamb chops cooked on the barbecue, washed down with cool-box beers.

Explore the steaming wonders of Rotorua

Come daybreak, the road squiggles north before reaching the spa town of Rotorua. Hunkered among silvery crater lakes of all shapes and sizes, the town is renowned for its sulphur-rich bathing waters and its fantastical Māori legends.

Rotorua's most memorable folk tales are told by 71-year-old Auntie Josie Scott, a Māori elder within the Ngāti Whakaue tribe. Storytelling is a big part of life in Rotorua, she explains, and few tell them better than her. She leads cultural walking tours around the historic settlement of Ohinemutu on the outskirts of Rotorua – by her reckoning, the most energized place on Earth.

'There's a magnetic strength that makes it impossible to leave,' she says, a geyser behind her letting off steam. 'The ground is alive, and that binds us here.' Strolling around the Māori village, past the cherry-red and white St Faith's Anglican Church, she points to outdoor bathing sheds and a thermal pool at the end of a neighbor's garden. 'It's 300 degrees in there,' she says. 'That heat is the lifeline that brought our tribe in the first place. Just don't get too close; you don't want to get any thermal activity on your buns.'

Rotorua has a complicated relationship with its waters – life here is not without its hazards. There are more than 1,200 hissing geothermal features in the area, and 500 pools and 65 geysers in the Whakarewarewa Valley alone. Hot springs can burst higher than a six-story building. Nevertheless, locals appreciate the tourism revenue they generate – there are daily crowds at meringue-shaped Lady Knox Geyser at Wai-O-Tapu, where plumes of froth surge skywards and steam vents from the ground, billowing across the hillside and blowing with an end-of-the-world fury.

Elsewhere in Wai-O-Tapu, the geysers – the wildest in the southern hemisphere – seem to dance and sing. Some squeak out bubbles, others blow cotton-candy puffs into the permanently sour-smelling air. There are lime-green cauldrons (whiffy eggs), scalloped-edge mud pools (week-old ham) and smoking caves (a gone-off bean fritter). In particular, the Champagne Pool makes unearthly gurgles, fizzing like the effervescent painkillers you might need after a night out on the good stuff.

The next day, the landscape turns from steamy to sun-kissed on the highway back to Auckland. For two hours the road rolls past forests, pastoral scenes and winding waterways. As the city at last rears into view and buildings close in around the campervan, attempting a last-minute U-turn feels like just the right thing to do.

How to get to Middle-earth

With the release of the first Lord of the Rings film 15 years ago, New Zealand was suddenly thrust on the travel radar for a whole new generation. Its beautiful landscapes from bubbling brooks to snow-capped peaks and lush forest valleys are the perfect setting for Peter Jackson's vision of Middle-earth, and now tourism is New Zealand's second largest industry.

The Hobbiton set is the country's best-known attraction today with close to half a million visitors a year, but there is of course a wealth of film locations far beyond 'the Shire'. You can always discover New Zealand's dramatic film locations (over 150 were used during filming) for yourself, starting with this handy guide, or you can head to this remote country on a tour.

We've rounded up a few of the many operators running Tolkien tours of New Zealand in 2017, each for a different type of travelers. One thing they all seem to have in common is the desire to meld real life with fantasy worlds while exploring one of the world's most beautiful countries.

Be a Middle-earth explorer

You can follow in the footsteps of Frodo and Bilbo with Round the World Experts (roundtheworldexperts.co.uk) on a 17-day tour of all things Lord of the Rings. As well as the obligatory visit to Hobbiton, the tour takes you to Wellington to go behind the scenes at the interactive Weta Cave workshops, learning how Lord of the Rings was brought to life with props, costumes, models and special effects. Next it's on to filming locations in the South Island, with highlights including exploring Aoraki (Mount Cook), New Zealand's highest mountain peak, discovering Queenstown, and experiencing the silence of Middle-earth on an overnight Milford Sound cruise

Wander windswept beaches

A 21-day tour with Discover the World (discover-the-world.co.uk) takes diehard fans through Lord of the Rings film locations with the national carrier, Air New Zealand (airnewzealand.com). The itinerary starts with a visit to Hobbiton in the rolling hills of Matamata, then hits all the visual splendor of the films, including the stunning beaches at the top of the South Island as well as the dramatic mountains and fjords of the Fiordland & Southland. There are several guided location tours included, as well as an overnight cruise on the spectacular Doubtful Sound.

Join the fellowship

Silverfern (silverfernholidays.com) does a 16-day journey travelling through New Zealand's magnificent landscapes from Auckland down to Queenstown. The tour includes film locations across the country, with a few surprises like dinner at the Green Dragon Inn in Hobbiton; and a hike to Pinnacle Ridge in the heights of Mount Ruapehu, which stands in for Mordor.

Lord it up on a luxury tour

Luxury travel outfit Zicasso (zicasso.com) covers similar territory but includes a private, after-hours tour of the Weta Cave as well as off-road adventures in a 4WD to Middle-earth film locations. A visit to the North Island is never complete without touring the steaming mud pools and erupting geysers at Rotorua's Wai-O-Tapu and Waimangu for more Lord of the Rings style photo opportunities. This guided tour then heads to the South Island to jet-boat past mountains and waterfalls on the glacier-fed Arrow River near Wanaka. Finally, take a helicopter ride over the Fox and Franz Josef and pretend you're flying over Caradhras, one of the three Mountains of Moria.

How to be a good 'freedom camper' in New Zealand

With diverse scenery packed into a compact country, and plenty of roads detouring to spectacular and remote locations, New Zealand is a brilliant place to experience a budget road-tripping and camping adventure. Of course, your respect for New Zealand's beaches, forests and waterways will also guarantee a friendly welcome from New Zealanders. Follow our top tips for a camping road trip so, in the local lingo, everything will be 'sweet as'.

Always ask first

Assume nothing, always ask at the local i-SITE tourist information center where you are allowed to 'freedom camp' (basically pull-up anywhere and set-up camp) in a local area. Yes, that stunning hilltop location you spotted when driving into town may well be privately owned and camping overnight means you'll be illegally trespassing on someone's land – with consequences!

Many New Zealand towns and cities offer free-of-charge designated areas where camping is allowed. Other places to check where camping is OK include Department of Conservation (DOC; doc.govt.nz) offices and holiday parks. Look out for – and do respect – signs indicating if camping is allowed or not.

DOC is your friend

Department of Conservation? These three words are your key to having a brilliant backpacking and road-tripping adventure throughout New Zealand. DOC manages more than 200 campsites around New Zealand, usually well-priced at just NZ$6 to NZ$10 per person per night, and these often include barbecues, cooking shelters, toilets and access to running water!

Top locations include alongside Lake Karapiro, just a short drive from Hobbiton on the North Island; and at Cascade Creek in the Fiordland National Park en route to the South Island's spectacular Milford Sound. DOC also operate free campsites, often in even more pristine wilderness areas of the country, but these are often restricted to fully self-contained vehicles only, as they often don't offer access to public toilets.

Get smart with that device

Add extra storage into your phone or tablet before you leave home. You're going to need it for your videos of Māori welcomes, mountain biking, and Milford Sound, but there are also a number of helpful apps worth downloading from Google Play or the Apple store. Produced in association with DOC and the i-SITE network, 'Official Camping NZ' shows every legal free-of-charge and paid camping location around the country. It's approved by every local council in NZ and reviews from other travelers on specific camping areas are included. Plus, you can download maps for offline use – a bonus as mobile internet data in New Zealand can be expensive. A similar app also worth downloading is CamperMate.

Hit the web

New Zealand's Tourism Industry Association has launched a 'Camping our way' website (camping.org.nz) with a handy 'Where to camp?' summary in English, French, Dutch, German and Spanish, and if you click on 'designated areas', a link appears to download the Official Camping NZ app. Easy.

To access the same regional camping information available on the app – including detailed descriptions of each location's facilities and costs and reviews from other travelers – head to the 'Respect NZ' map on the Rankers website (rankers.co.nz/respect). And if you're hiring a campervan from local companies including Spaceships (spaceshipsrentals.co.nz), Jucy Rentals (jucy.co.nz) or Escape (escaperentals.co.nz), their websites also feature freedom camping guidelines. Basically there is plenty of information out there on how to freedom camp in New Zealand.

The importance of on-board toilet facilities

Read this very carefully if you're planning on camping around New Zealand... If you're driving a campervan with toilet facilities including an on-board grey water storage system, you are allowed to stop and stay at authorized campsites without public toilets. (Note that dumping facilities for waste water are mapped on various camping websites and smartphone apps.)

If you're driving a smaller campervan or are in an ordinary car, camping is only allowed at campsites where public toilets are provided. Why? Well the answer is probably pretty obvious: New Zealand won't be beautiful forever if its strewn with used toilet paper now, will it?

Be environmentally aware

Kiwis – both the easygoing locals and the country's feathered, long-beaked national bird – are fiercely proud of their nation, and love to share their home with visitors. Unfortunately, their love and respect for the South Pacific home has not always been reciprocated by some travelers and this is causing a fair bit of angst in New Zealand these days. By following the guidelines you'll have a much better, and less environmentally damaging, freedom camping trip around the country.

Leave no trace of your campsite.

Properly dispose of all your litter. If there are no bins, take it with you.

Don't chop down trees and vegetation for campfires – unbelievably this has been done by some clueless campers in New Zealand across recent years. Really.

When cleaning or washing, be sure to keep soaps, detergents and toothpaste out of the waterways.

Travellers come all this way to experience New Zealand's world-beating environment, and it's our shared responsibility to treat the country's forests, lakes and rivers with kindness and respect.

Sorry, it's the law

Sadly, due to the actions of some freedom campers around New Zealand over the last decade – including leaving rubbish and used toilet paper on beaches, roadsides and in bushes (!) – the country passed the Freedom Camping Act in 2011.

This means local councils have the authority to fine anyone camping overnight illegally up to NZ$200 per vehicle. A few local authorities also add a further NZ$200 wheel-clamping fee. That spur-of-the-moment decision to spend the night camped illegally on a lake's edge does have the potential to get expensive, and yes there are plans afoot to ensure fines are paid before you leave New Zealand.

With a wide range of free-of-charge and low-cost camping options available, and plenty of information available on how and where to access these, fines are a tough but fair punishment that have wide support from New Zealanders.

We advise: love this country like the locals do, and enjoy your freedom camping trip around this gorgeous country. Sweet as.

New Zealand's secret paradise: the best of Taranaki

Tucked away on the central west coast of New Zealand's North Island, the Taranaki region is both overlooked and under-appreciated. But for more intrepid travelers, the area dubbed 'the 'Naki' is definitely worth a detour.

It's a region of rolling dairy farms, easygoing residents and sleepy side roads, but look further and you'll find black-sand beaches whipped by Tasman Sea surf, and a provincial capital with a surprising world-class arts scene. Looming over the whole landscape is Mt Taranaki – one of New Zealand's most photogenic mountains.

Art meets nature in New Plymouth

Art and nature complement each other in Taranaki's capital, New Plymouth. The spectacular Wind Wand – a towering kinetic sculpture designed by New Zealand artist Len Lye – arcs and sways in staunch breezes surging in from the Tasman Sea, while the mirror-clad folds of the recently opened Len Lye Centre shimmer with southern hemisphere sunshine and shape-shifting clouds. Nearby, 19th-century heritage buildings offer an intriguing contrast.

One of the 20th century's most interesting artists, Lye opined that 'Great art goes 50-50 with great architecture', and the ratio at the center gets the balance exactly right. Towering ceilings create a sense of space and drama, while ramps lead visitors through galleries of Lye's challenging kinetic structures and boldly energetic films. Sculptures whir and buzz and Lye's color-drenched or starkly monochrome short films shimmy and shake. Welcome to one of the noisiest and exciting galleries on the planet.

Adjoining the Len Lye Centre is the Govett-Brewster Art Gallery, renowned as one of New Zealand's best regional art galleries. With a motto of 'Provocateurs since 1970' the gallery focuses on experimental and challenging local and international exhibitions. In a region traditionally more attuned to dairy farming and laid-back surfers hunting the perfect wave, this is another of Taranaki's best-kept secrets.

In mid-March, sleepy New Plymouth effortlessly morphs into the southern hemisphere's world music hotspot. Every year the WOMAD festival fills the city's TBS Bowl of Brooklands in Pukekura Park for a few exciting days. Recent festivals have included South African township a capella harmonies, Spanish flamenco beats and thumping Romany trumpet and tuba ensembles from the Balkans.

Outdoor adventures and foodie treats

In a land renowned for its iconic hiking, the Pouakai Crossing – the route around the perfect volcanic cone of Mt Taranaki – is an Instagram-worthy contender for the country's finest one-day walk.

Traversing the northern side of the mountain, the 19km trek (seven to nine hours walking) negotiates diverse landscapes from forest through to sub-alpine scrub, and includes waterfalls, alpine tarns and swamps. There are also much lower visitor numbers than other more well-known hikes. Top Guides offers guided walks, shuttle transport and other shorter half-day excursions on sections of the Crossing.

After a day outdoors, it's just a short hop to return to New Plymouth and its excellent dining scene. Kick off at The Hour Glass, one of the country's best craft beer bars – look for beers from Taranaki locals Brew Mountain (brewmountain.co.nz) or Mike's Brewery – before tucking into robust charcoal-grilled dishes at Social Kitchen (social-kitchen.co.nz).

Other day trips to consider over your Taranaki pork belly include a 20-minute vertiginous scramble up Paritutu (154m) at the southern end of town, or for something more accessible, a forest walk around the Dawson Falls area on the eastern slopes of Mt Taranaki.

Roadtripping Surf Highway 45

Get some Kiwi tunes on your playlist before embarking on this 105km semi-circular route from New Plymouth to Hawera. At Oakura, the world's biggest surfboard stands outside Butler's Reef Hotel (butlersreef.co.nz) – during summer the pub's raffish beer garden hosts standing-room-only gigs from NZ's biggest bands – while the hip Kin & Co (facebook.com/KinandCo) cafe dispenses organic and artisan flavors with a side order of tattooed barista.

Along the route there are plenty of spots to plant your board. The black sand- and driftwood-adorned Ahu Ahu beach is the last resting place of the SS Gairloch, now a rusted skeleton in the waves after foundering on

Timaru Reef in 1903. On the horizon, the soaring profile of Paritutu can be spied, while the constant and comforting presence of Mt Taranaki rises behind forested hills.

Travelling southwest of Warea, keep your eyes peeled for a Taranaki landmark: a huge boulder daubed with orange paint that announces the route to legendary surf break, Stent Rd – the original yellow road marker kept getting stolen by trophy-hunting surfers.

Less than 40km from New Plymouth's art-infused vibe, the Tasman shoreline here feels wonderfully remote, as the indigo ocean dissolves into the horizon. Take a turning down Cape Rd near Pungarehu for a rolling landscape of gassy and bizarre lahar mounds, which are testament to the area's explosive volcanic past. At the end of the road is the century-old Cape Egmont lighthouse.

Further south, Opunake is a town dotted with heritage buildings and colorful murals – say 'G'day' to the friendly team at Opunake Fish Chips & More (facebook.com/Opunakefishchipsandmore) as you're ordering lunch – before cruising on to Hawera where the excellent Tawhiti Museum tells the story of traders, whalers and NZ's indigenous Māori people. One final Surf Highway experience is climbing the 215 steps of Hawera's water tower for glimpses of Mt Taranaki's graceful volcanic cone and the surf-fringed coastline prescribing this surprising region.

Getting inked in New Zealand: a history

Tattoos have been a part of human history for thousands of years, taking many forms of style and practice. While they have faced varying degrees of social acceptance in different places, tattoos are undoubtedly part of the mainstream today.

New Plymouth might seem like an unlikely place for an international tattoo exhibition, but in November this hip little coastal town attracts some of the world's most sought-after artists to the New Zealand Tattoo & Art Festival, adding to the country's already storied history of tattooing.

The Māori moko

For the Māori, the indigenous people of New Zealand, the tattoo tradition of the Tā moko is a sacred part of cultural identity. Before the arrival of the Europeans, receiving one's moko was a significant rite of passage, marking the transition from childhood to adulthood and indicating social status. Traditional Māori tattooist carved intricate designs onto the skin using a tool called the uhi, a chisel that creates the unique scarring effect that sets the moko apart from other styles of Polynesian tattooing.

Historically, moko has been worn by both genders. For men, bold full-face tattoos communicated important aspects of the wearer's identity – their rank, lineage, and tribe were all represented – and the designs were often memorized and used as signatures. Men also wore puhoro, elaborate, swirling tattoos stretching from the torso to the knees, to enhance physical attractiveness. Women most commonly wore a variation called moko kauae on their lips and chin, which similarly signifies important information about the wearer's life.

When large numbers of English colonists arrived in the second half of the 19th century, they attempted to oppress Māori culture and practices – people were punished for speaking Māori and moko actively discouraged. However, like other forms of tattooing, moko has experienced a resurgence in popularity; while artists more often complete the designs with a tattoo gun than an uhi, the sacred designs remain an important symbol of Māori cultural identity and resistance.

In 1873, Czech artist Gottfried Lindauer became fascinated by Māori body art, painting over 100 portraits of Māori people. One of the most detailed historic records of moko ever produced, this collection is housed at the Auckland Art Gallery.

Artsy New Plymouth

New Plymouth was already known in New Zealand for its quirky art and festivals scene. It's host to Womad (womad.co.nz) – arguably New Zealand's best music festival – every March, so a tattoo festival seems a natural addition to the local calendar.

Among the city's other diverse cultural offerings there's the Len Lye Center, housed in one of New Zealand's more playfully designed buildings, which gives visitors a crash course in Mr. Lye's postmodern visions via his collection of experimental films and kinetic sculptures. Neighbouring Govett-Brewster Art Gallery hosts a wide range of contemporary local and international shows. And for those looking for a little outdoor whimsy, Pukekura Park turns into an electric wonderland every summer during its psychedelic Festival of Lights (festivaloflights.nz).

So you want a new tattoo?

Known as Australasia's biggest tattoo event, the New Zealand Tattoo and Art Festival (nztattooart.com) is in its sixth year, featuring an impressive roster of artists from around the globe specializing in all styles of tattooing. Some of the big names at this year's festival include Tommy Helm (empirestatestudios.com), Megan Massacre (meganmassacre.com), Jesse Smith (facebook.com) and Teressa Sharpe (teresasharpeart.com).

While tattoo appointments for the festival need to be directly booked with the individual artists, some take walk-up clients, should you feel like spontaneously taking the plunge into the world of permanent body art.

For those who are more interested in checking out quality ink and mingling with other enthusiasts, the festival will also be hosting a number of entertainment acts, including freestyle motocross and BMX shows, a skating competition, as well as aerial and fire dancing performances. Already tatted up and ready to show off your art? See how your ink stacks up in the event's annual tattoo competition.

In 2016 the festival will be taking place on November 26 & 27 at New Plymouth's TSB Stadium. Adult single day passes are available for $25 in advance and $30 at the door, while two-day passes are available for presale at $40 and will $50 the day of the event. Kids under the age of 14 can attend the festival free of charge.

From geometric patterns to splashy watercolor pieces to traditional American sailor designs, ink is no longer a trend. It's here to stay, permanently.

New Zealand's best foodie events

New Zealand's fresh produce, artisan producers, top-notch wines and a lively craft beer scene make it a mouth-watering destination for discerning foodies. And best of all, it's easy for visitors to enjoy these at a slew of tempting food, wine and beer festivals that offer a chance to sample regional gourmet treats and tasty tipples, often amid jaw-dropping scenery.

Whether you want a big slick city extravaganza or a small town cook-up, New Zealand's food festival calendar offers plenty to plan your trip around. Here is our wrap-up of the best ways to tempt your taste buds by the season.

Summer (December, January, February)

Summer's the time to kick back and head to the beach. If you're road-tripping pop a chilly bin (ice box) in the back of the car to cram with goodies ready for a picnic or barbecue. Look out for roadside veggie vans with the freshest sweetcorn, peaches, nectarines and luscious juicy strawberries. The Bay of Plenty is the top spot for straight-from-the-orchard avocados while down in Otago the cherries are plump, glossy and bursting with flavor. And after a day basking in the sun what better way to cool down than with a 'hokey pokey' ice cream.

Central Otago Pinot Noir Celebration (January)

Queenstown sits in the center of prime pinot noir country with the schist soil the perfect terroir for producing a top drop amid awe-inspiring scenery. (pinotcelebration.co.nz)

New Zealand National Cherry Spitting Championships (January)

Cromwell in Central Otago is the fruit bowl of New Zealand and for this one day it's no place for good manners. So, if you think you can spit a cherry stone more than 11 meters, now is your chance. (cromwell.org.nz)

Kawhia Moana, Kawhia Kai, Kawhia Tangata Festival (February)

The tiny North Island town of Kawhia welcomes all to celebrate Maori food and culture. You will get the chance to try traditional hangi (food cooked in a pit heated by hot stones), then see Maori crafts such as flax weaving or wood carving, and kapa haka groups performing traditional songs, chanting and dance. (facebook.com/kawhiakai)

Ocean & Orchard Food & Wine Festival (February)

Simply fabulous: fabulous food, fabulous wine, fabulous music… you get the picture of Kerikeri's best day out. (oceanandorchardfestival.co.nz)

Marlborough Wine & Food Festival (February)

Prepare to be wowed by the crisp sauvignon blancs that Marlborough is famous for. Set among the vines at the area's oldest vineyard this is a true favorite on the fine food calendar. (wine-marlborough-festival.co.nz)

Autumn (March, April, May)

It's harvest time in the vineyards and orchards and in backyards all over the country the feijoa trees are laden. These egg-sized fruit have a bubble gummy flavor, usually described as blend of pineapple, strawberry and guava. Down in Bluff, at the bottom of the South Island, it's time to eat oysters.

Great Kiwi Beer Festival (March)

Cheers! Christchurch hosts New Zealand's hippest hop festival showcasing the vibrant craft beer scene, with suitably beery food and groovy tunes. (greatkiwibeerfestival.co.nz)

Waiheke Vintage Festival (April)

Just a ferry ride from Auckland, gorgeous Waiheke Island entices wine and food fans for two weekends of food, wine and music hosted by a clutch of the island's boutique wineries. (waihekevintagefestival.co.nz)

Bluff Oyster Festival (May)

Bluff oysters grow slowly in the pristine cold waters of the Fouveaux Strait to big, briny deliciousness. If you tire of oysters there's an abundance of other seafood and local specialties including mutton bird, and great southern ales. (bluffoysterfest.co.nz)

Hokitika Wildfoods Festival (March)

One for the intrepid eater, there's weird and wild fare to try in Hokitika: beetles, mountain oysters and the infamous stallion shakes. Go on, have a chocolate-covered huhu grub – you know you want to. (wildfoods.co.nz)

Winter (June, July, August)

Wellington woos guests in winter with a swag of festivals, and while you're there why not check out the windy city's cafe scene where coffee connoisseurs can swoon over cold drip, pour over or syphon. If you're hanging with the snow-bunnies for the ski season it's a cool time to check out the boutique breweries' rich malty winter ales at a local festival, or head to the pub, order a pint and cheer on the All Blacks.

SOBA Winter Ale Festival (June)

Wellington taps the brew masters' wintery ales at this celebration of all things beer. (soba.org.nz)

Cadbury Chocolate Carnival (July)

Two things you may not know about Dunedin: its Cadbury factory makes jaffas (small candy-covered chocolate balls); it has the steepest street in the world. The week-long carnival culminates with 30,000 giant jaffas hurtling down Baldwin Street. Sweet as! (cadbury.co.nz)

Wellington on a Plate (August)

Two weeks of one-off events, pop-ups, walks, tours and festival-special restaurant menus in Wellington. (wellingtononaplate.com)

Beervana (August)

Once again Wellington releases your inner beer geek at New Zealand's biggest craft beer get-together. (beervana.co.nz)

Spring (September, October, November)

As the weather warms up farmers' markets are revitalized with spring greens and tender asparagus. On the west coast of the South Island it's whitebait season. Don't miss the whitebait fritters, tiny translucent fish are whisked with eggs then fried quickly until crisp.

Whitianga Scallop Festival (September)

The glorious coastal region of the Coromandel celebrates the new season's scallops and seafood. (scallopfestival.co.nz)

Kaikoura Seafest (October)

'Kai' means food in Maori and 'koura' means crayfish. Kaikoura Seafest plates up seafood galore – think crayfish, green-lipped mussels and scallops, just for starters. Add local beer and local bands for a seriously memorable Kiwi experience. (seafest.co.nz)

Toast Martinborough (November)

A stone's throw from Wellington, the lovely village of Martinborough puts on a spread with vintages matched with restaurant-quality food and live music. (toastmartinborough.co.nz)

Food & Wine Classic Summer (November)

The festival motto is 'make sure you come hungry' for ten days of gourmet food and wine events around Hawke's Bay, New Zealand's oldest wine producing area. Also hosts a winter event in June. (fawc.co.nz).

Ten stunning New Zealand cycle rides

It looks like New Zealand's cycling revolution is set to keep rolling, with stacks of new tracks opening and walking trails being converted to dual use. Unsurprisingly, travelers have been quick to cotton on, encouraged by bike hire and shuttle services in all the right places. Offering opportunities to see so much in so little time, with the bonus of fresh air and exercise, these day rides are an unbeatable way to go exploring.

Karangahake Gorge

This is the most picturesque and interesting section of the Hauraki Rail Trail, which follows an old railway line at the base of Coromandel Peninsula. Highlights of Karangahake Gorge include photogenic gold mining relics and the freaky Windows Walkway, but the pièce de résistance is an amazing 1100-metre long railway tunnel, which you wobble through with the help of a torch. Head into the gorge from Waikino Station, site of the bike hire depot and a quaint cafe.

The Redwoods

Rotorua's 5000-hectare Whakarewarewa Forest – known as the Redwoods – is a New Zealand mountain biking mecca, with more than

100km of trails ranging from sedate to positively treacherous. Head to Waipa Mill car park for bike hire and advice on which of the zillions of options you should choose. The 'Inner Core' area offers fun mountain bike riding for beginners and families; another option is to cruise along easy forestry trails to the picnic area at Blue Lake.

Huka Falls Trails

These riverside trails make a full and fun day out of visiting Huka Falls. The Rotary Ride starts in Taupo's thermal Spa Park and follows an undulating path along the Waikato River. The river is bridged at the thunderous Huka Falls viewing point, where riders can linger before heading back along the other side via the Redwood Track. The ride can be extended by continuing beyond the Falls to Aratiatia Dam, or heading up into Craters of the Moon Mountain Bike Park (greatlaketaupo.com).

Old Coach Road

This 15km trail follows an historic coach road around Mt Ruapehu's forested foothills, largely forgotten and overgrown until restored by the locals. Gently graded with the occasional climb, it passes unique engineering features including two handsome viaducts. Creative interpretation panels retell stories from times past, and there are various viewpoints around the volcanic plateau. Shuttle services run riders and bikes out to Horopito, from where it's mostly downhill back to Ohakune.

Puketapu Loop

One of the country's best year-round cycling destinations due to friendly weather and terrain, Hawke's Bay now boasts an enviable 187km network of cycle ways ranging from riverside stop banks to quiet country roads and coastal paths. Starting at Taradale, on the edge of Napier, the Puketapu Loop is a goody, following the Tutaekuri River up one side and back down the other, with stunning rural and vineyard views, and the bonus of the rural Puketapu Pub (thepuketapu.co.nz) at the halfway point.

Great Taste Trail

This tasteful trail takes in wine, food and art as it loops through the Nelson region's picturesque countryside and along the coast. The section from Motueka to Kaiteriteri serves up a delightful assortment, passing fruit stalls, cafes and a craft brewery on its way along quiet lanes and orchard roads. Emerging from the fruitlands, the trail follows a coastal cycle way before entering Kaiteriteri Mountain Bike Park. Tasman Bay views and the glorious golden sands and swimming at Kaiteriteri Beach make the gentle climb worthwhile.

Queen Charlotte Track

One of 22 national Great Rides, the 70km Queen Charlotte Track is a magnet for intermediate cyclists who complete it in two days. Those looking for a day trip can enjoy many of its Marlborough Sounds' views by starting at Torea Saddle and riding through to Anakiwa, with the option of a scenic detour along the road to reduce the overall effort. Highlights include the boat cruise to get there, sweeping downhills, sweet-smelling beech forest, and a series of bays including Mistletoe where you can jump off the jetty.

West Coast Wilderness Trail

This 120km trail from Greymouth to Ross retraces the paths left by pioneering packhorses, trams and trains, with new routes forged to link them. The result is a trail revealing spectacular vistas of dense rainforest, glacial rivers, lakes and wetlands, as well as the snow-capped Southern Alps and the wild Tasman Sea. A leisurely ride can be had from Greymouth, along the Tasman Sea coast with dunes and lagoons, along a tram line though regenerating bush and farmland to Kumara, site of the beautifully restored Theatre Royal Hotel.

Arrow River Bridges Trail

The 100km Queenstown Trails range from easy lakeside jaunts to cross-country treks. This one is the latter, starting at Arrowtown and following the Arrow River, crossing five bridges and spying picture-postcard cottages along quiet country lanes. Having skirted a gorge, the trail meets the AJ Hackett Bungy center at historic Kawarau Bridge. Celebrate your big bounce with bubbles at Chard Farm winery before being collected by shuttle.

Roxburgh Gorge Trail

With its magnificent backdrop of golden, rolling ranges, Central Otago is a candidate for New Zealand's most scenic cycling destination. One of many notable trails, the 34km Roxburgh Gorge offers a spectacular ride along the Clutha River between Alexandra and the Roxburgh Dam. After riding the rocky gorge with its towering bluffs, the trail eventually emerges into an historic gold mining area. From there, riders hop on a jet boat and zip 12km downriver before re-mounting their steeds to complete the journey through to the Dam.

New Zealand's unmissable aquatic adventures

With the world's tenth longest coastline and an interior riven with more than 180,000km of charted rivers, it's no surprise that New Zealand's cup is overflowing with watery adventures. Surfing, kayaking, rafting, diving, snorkeling, sailing, and even swimming with dolphins or seals, there's plenty to immerse yourself in.

Diving the Poor Knights

Poor Knights marine reserve, off Northland's east coast, was rated by aquatic legend Jacques Cousteau as one of the world's top 10 diving spots. The island's underwater cliffs drop steeply through crystal waters to form a maze of archways, caves and tunnels adorned with sponges and a vivid array of underwater vegetation. Rays, and a variety of colorful fish not present elsewhere in New Zealand, can be spotted here thanks to the subtropical current from the Coral Sea.

Surfing Raglan

Sweet and salty little Raglan is surfing central, with serious waxheads heading to Manu Bay, rumored to have the world's longest left-hand break. Mere mortals are best kicking things off at beautiful Ngarunui (raglan23.co.nz), with less forbidding waves and lifeguard patrol (October to April). Hang ten with the friendly Raglan Surfing School (raglansurfingschool.co.nz), where they pride themselves on getting 95% of first-timers standing during their lesson. The beach is also great for swimming and sunsets.

Sailing Auckland

Join professional sailors on a real America's Cup yacht and go racing around Auckland's scenic Waitemata Harbor (exploregroup.co.nz). Go head to head with another crew and grind, tack and gybe your way on the windward course with the Auckland city skyline as your backdrop. Everyone gets a go at taking the helm, although landlubbers have the option of just shooting the breeze, sitting back and watching your teammates do all the hard work.

Blackwater rafting in Waitomo

Waitomo Caves are a subterranean wonderland filled with peculiar formations and galaxies of glowworms that can be explored on a Legendary Black Water Rafting trip (waitomo.com/black-water-rafting). Don a wetsuit, abseil into the abyss and then squeeze, climb and slide your way through the limestone labyrinth before floating through a glowworm-lit passage on a rubber inner-tube. You'll have so much fun, you'll forget that you're underground.

Tongariro River Rafting

Touted by anglers as one of the best trout fishing rivers in the world, the Tongariro also hooks its fair share of thrill-seekers keen to paddle their way down more than 60 roller coaster rapids as the river wends its way through ancient beech forest. Test the waters with a gentle Family Float, splash into the grade III white water or take on a more physical kayak trip with local outfit Tongariro River Rafting (trr.co.nz). On the river, keep an eye out for whio; these rare whistling blue ducks are excellent swimmers.

Kayaking in Abel Tasman National Park

At the top of the South Island is Abel Tasman National Park, a heavenly stretch of indented coastline where golden sands and forest fringes are lapped by cerulean waters. You can walk the 51km coastal track (doc.govt.nz), but paddle power is a lot more rock 'n' roll. Kayaking operators will provide gear and guides, and you can choose anything from a sunset paddle to a three-day catered camping affair, or combine kayaking with walking a stretch of the track and boat cruises. Secret cove and desert-island fantasies beckon.

Canyoning in the Torrent River

Drawn in by sparkling seas, peachy beaches and quintessential coastal forest, few visitors to Abel Tasman actually get to explore the park's rugged interior and untouched river systems. Here's your chance with Abel Tasman Canyons. Journey down the beautiful granite-lined Torrent River canyon via a fun-filled combination of swimming, sliding, abseiling and lofty leaps into jewel-like pools. It's like some kind of unruly, over-sized water park, but much better looking and a thousand times more fun.

Swimming with seals in Kaikoura

World-famous for whale watching, Kaikoura is also a top destination for swimming with New Zealand fur seals. Watch adolescents spin and dive amid tangles of kelp, while curious pups make underwater eye contact with wet-suited interlopers. Seal Swim Kaikoura's two-hour guided snorkeling tours (October to May) were named one of the world's best marine encounters by Lonely Planet in 2013.

Kayaking the Okarito Lagoon

Seaside hamlet Okarito (with a lucky population of 30-ish) sits alongside its namesake lagoon – the largest unmodified wetland in New Zealand. It's an excellent place for spotting birds like the rare kiwi and majestic kotuku (great white heron). Okarito Nature Tours hire out kayaks for guided and unguided paddles on the lagoon and up into the luxuriant rainforest channels where all sorts of birds hang out. On a good day, the impressive Southern Alps provide a distracting backdrop.

Scenic day-long hikes: walking in New Zealand

New Zealand may be justifiably famous for its Great Walks and other multi-day hiking trails, but don't break out the cooking stove and sleeping bag just yet. Much of the same wilderness can be explored on day hikes, which means less gear, less effort, and quite possibly more fun.

1. Twilight–Te Werahi Loop

This five-hour loop provides a front-row view of the Far North's natural drama, starring powerful seas, shifting sands, shapely headlands and ever-changing light. The track (doc.govt.nz) is mostly flat and easy-going, as it meanders between vast beaches and coastal forest. Combine the hike with a pilgrimage to windswept Cape Reinga (Te Rerenga

Wairua), where the swirling waters of the Tasman Sea and Pacific Ocean meet, and Maori spirits are said to depart for the afterlife.

2. Rangitoto Island Loop

Auckland's youngest but largest volcanic cone was created just 600 years ago in a series of fiery eruptions. It is an elegant island and beloved city icon, reachable via a short ferry ride from downtown Auckland. Hike up the modest summit (250m) for great views of the city, before wandering along the coast where hardy plants pursue their quest to populate the lava fields. Surprisingly, Rangitoto is home to the country's largest pohutukawa forest.

3. Coromandel Walkway

The remote and rugged tip of the Coromandel Peninsula is well worth the time and effort required to reach it, particularly if you soak up its superlative scenery on the coastal Coromandel Walkway (doc.govt.nz). Linking Stony Bay and Fletcher Bay, the 10km track takes three or four hours, with memorable views over the aptly named Sugar Loaf, Pinnacles and Great Barrier Island. A whole day is required to complete the return hike, or you can arrange shuttle transport with Coromandel Discovery (coromandeldiscovery.com).

4. Tongariro Alpine Crossing

Set amongst volcanic scenery made famous by The Lord of the Rings trilogy, this crossing (doc.govt.nz) in Tongariro National Park is often lauded as New Zealand's finest one-day walk and one of the best in the world. It's no wonder, with its peculiar moonscape graced with steaming vents and springs, vivid lakes and vast ridges. The highly weather-dependent 20km walk takes between six and eight hours, although sure-footed types can add on a side-trip up the near-perfect cone of Mt Ngauruhoe (aka Mt Doom).

5. Medlands Beach to Anchorage

This 11km section of the Abel Tasman Coastal Track serves up several stretches of beach paradise, swathed in golden sand and awash with sparkling sea. The easy trail linking them wends through Abel Tasman National Park's lush, ferny coastal forest with lots of lovely lookout points. Getting there involves a super-scenic boat cruise, and you can also combine your walk with a kayak trip. Another appealing option is to linger at idyllic Anchorage and make the side-trip to magical Cleopatra's Pool.

6. Mt Robert Circuit

If bagging a summit is on your wish-list, this trail in Nelson Lakes National Park is a great place to start. It zigzags up the aptly named Pinchgut Track on to Mt Robert, with beautiful Lake Rotoiti in view for much of the way. If time allows and the weather is kind, the side-trip along Robert Ridge towards Lake Angelus is irresistible, and rewards with expansive mountain vistas into the heart of the park. Amble back down via the gentler Paddy's Track to complete the four- to five-hour circuit (doc.govt.nz).

7. Sealy Tarns

Home to more than three-quarters of New Zealand's highest mountains, Aoraki (Mt Cook) National Park's vertiginous terrain is generally more suited to climbers than hikers. However, a number of trails offer the chance to survey this majestic landscape, all starting from the excellent National Park Visitor Centre. Our pick is Sealy Tarns Track, and although it involves a grunty, two-hour climb, the ever-present views of the Hooker Valley and surrounding peaks should provide ample distractions.

8. Avalanche Peak

This challenging circuit track clambers to the summit of Avalanche Peak (1833m), which looms dramatically over Arthur's Pass village (doc.govt.nz). Views of the surrounding mountains, valleys and hanging

97

glaciers in Arthur's Pass National Park may well bring a tear to your eye, although that might just be the near-1100m ascent to the crumbly summit. This summer-only trip takes between six and eight hours, and it isn't for the faint-hearted. The steeper Avalanche Peak Track is the quickest way up, while the descent via Scotts Track is easier on the knees.

9. Charming Creek Walkway

One of the best day-walks on the West Coast, the Charming Creek Walkway (doc.govt.nz) is an all-weather trail following an old coal railway line through the Ngakawau River gorge. Along its length (about six hours return) are rusty relics, tunnels, a suspension bridge, fascinating geological formations, and the mighty Mangatini Falls. The walkway is also an excellent mountain bike ride. Ask locals about transport to avoid retracing your steps.

10. Key Summit

This three-hour return hike (doc.govt.nz) offers a taste of the Routeburn Track, arguably the most scenic of New Zealand's Great Walks (greatwalks.co.nz). Starting from the Milford Sound Road, it climbs steadily beyond the bushline, into an alpine wonderland of tarns, sphagnum bogs, stunted beech trees and spiky dracophyllum plants. The summit walkway affords panoramic views of Fiordland National Park's mountains, valleys and waterfalls, and completes the picture with interpretive displays explaining how this spectacular landscape was formed.

New Zealand's 10 most unforgettable beaches

With 15,000 kilometers of coastline, New Zealand is heaven for beach-lovers. Its diverse shores dish up everything from lazy days and blazing sunsets, to active adventures such as swimming, kayaking and surfing. Finding a great beach is easy; to find an unforgettable one, read on...

Ninety Mile Beach

It's a poorly kept secret that Ninety Mile Beach is in fact only 88km, but there's no way you'll feel short-changed here. Starting near Kaitaia and ending close to Cape Reinga (Te Rerenga Wairua) – New Zealand's spiritual northern point – it's an epic expanse of sand and endless ocean, backed by massive dunes that are guaranteed to put sand in your pants.

Just shy of the Cape is Te Paki Stream car park. A walkway from here leads to the beach and northwards to Scott Point.

Piha

The popular TV show Piha Rescue follows the heroics of this beach's busy surf-lifesaving crew. But while Piha is infamous for unruly surf and strong undertows, it well deserves its mantle as Auckland's most popular seaside playground. Sizzle yourself on its hot black sand, frolic amid foamy white rollers (always swim between the flags), and wander the beach and surrounding walking tracks to better admire the shapely headlands of Lion Rock and Taitomo Island.

New Chums Beach

Beautiful beaches are ten a penny on the Coromandel Peninsula, but New Chums stands out for its isolation. It's actually only half an hour's walk from Whangapoua car park, but such is the rock-hopping and scampering required that many don't even attempt it. The reward is a beach so golden, a sea so glittering, pohutukawa trees so gnarled (and resplendent in red blooms around Christmas), that its beauty may bring a tear to your eye. What's more, you might have it all to yourself.

Ngarunui

Sweet and salty little Raglan is waxhead central, with serious surfers heading to Manu Bay, rumored to have the world's longest left-hand break. Mere mortals are better off at nearby Ngarunui (raglan23.co.nz), where friendlier surf allows for safer swimming, even more so from October to April when the beach is patrolled by lifeguards. It's a busy and entertaining place on fine, summer days, especially when the grommets of Raglan Surf School are giving this surfing lark a go. Could that be you?

Wainui, Eastland

Meaning 'big water' in Maori, it's no surprise that New Zealand has more Wainuis than you can poke an oar at. Just up the coast from Gisborne, this Wainui is a cracker: it offers great swimming and a quality surf break, backed by a series of dune and bush reserves. Wainui sustains a close-knit community of ocean-lovers including stalwarts of the surf-lifesaving club, as well as Wainui Store which fries up good fish and chips.

Anchorage

Picking the best beach in Abel Tasman National Park isn't easy, for its coastline boasts one stunner after another. Anchorage stakes a strong claim not only for its sheer natural beauty – a gently sloping arc of golden sand, fringed with lush forest – but also for its access to a stunning stretch of the coastal Great Walk. It's possible to overnight in the conservation campsite or hut, which should allow time to take the short side-trip to magical Cleopatra's Pool.

Scott's Beach

The coastal crescendo of Kahurangi National Park's multi-day Heaphy Track, this remote beach can also be reached from the northern extremity of the West Coast Road. And what a journey it is: the intensely scenic drive through Karamea to Kohaihai, the end-of-the-line camping reserve in a magnificent estuary setting. From there you can venture into the national park, over a low hill to Scott's Beach. Likely to be shrouded in a salt mist, the beguiling scene features jagged rocks, nikau palm forest, and powerful waves clawing at the driftwood-strewn beach.

Wharariki

Brace yourself for an eye-popping surprise after the 20-minute farm walk in western Golden Bay. Boom! Mighty dunes lead down to a wild, West Coast sea. Jagged rock islands stand firm in the shallows, smashed by the waves. Seals may be seen scampering. Light shimmers across wet, rippled sands. Wharariki Beach is too dangerous for swimming so don't bother with the beach towel. But do try to time your visit for early morning or late afternoon, and definitely bring your camera.

Sumner

Tucked around the corner, 10km from central Christchurch, the bright and breezy seaside suburb of Sumner dishes up a classic day at the beach. It's a popular spot for locals, who turn up en masse bringing with them an upbeat, holiday vibe. The sandy beach bustles with swimmers and surfers (and lifeguards), while the village's cafes and restaurants churn out ice cream, coffee and burgers at a rapid rate of knots.

Purakaunui Bay

Sixteen kilometers from the nearest town (Owaka, population 300), this is a genuine hidden gem in a super-sleepy corner of The Catlins, Southland. It has few claims to fame, save a small (and CGI) role in The Lion, the Witch and the Wardrobe – totally overshadowed by those volcanoes in The Lord of the Rings. And hooray for that, because Purakaunui is all about peace and quiet. It's a lovely beach, framed by high cliffs, with pockets of native bush and a large grassy reserve. There's blissfully little to do, except swimming when the surf's off, and surfing when it's on.

Sights in New Zealand

Blue Penguin Colony

Bird sanctuary in Oamaru

Hours - 10am until 2hr after sunset

Contact - http://www.penguins.co.nz; 03-433 1195

Location - 2 Waterfront Rd, Oamaru, New Zealand

Every evening the little tykes from the Oamaru little-penguin colony surf in and wade ashore, heading to their nests in an old stone quarry near the waterfront. Stands are set up on either side of the waddle route. General admission (adult/child $28/14) will give you a good view of the action but the premium stand ($40/20), accessed by a boardwalk through the nesting area, will get you closer.

You'll see the most penguins (up to 250) in November and December. From March to August there may be only 10 to 50 birds. They arrive in clumps called rafts just before dark (around 5.30pm in midwinter and 9.30pm midsummer), and it takes them about an hour to all come ashore; nightly viewing times are posted at the i-SITE. Use of cameras is prohibited and you're advised to dress warmly.

To understand the centre's conservation work and its success in increasing the penguin population, take the daytime, behind-the-scenes tour (adult/child self-guided $10/5 or guided $16/8); packages that combine night viewing and the daytime tour are available.

Do not under any circumstances wander around the rocks beside the sea here at night looking for penguins. It's damaging to their environment and spoils studies into the human effects on the birds.

Victorian Precinct

Top choice area in Oamaru

Location - Oamaru, New Zealand

Consisting of only a couple of blocks centered on Harbor and Tyne Sts, this atmospheric enclave has some of NZ's best-preserved Victorian commercial buildings. Descend on a dark and foggy night and it's downright Dickensian. It's also ground zero for all that is hip, cool and freaky in Oamaru, and one of the most fun places to window-shop in the entire South Island.

Wander around during the day and you'll discover antiquarian bookshops, antique stores, galleries, vintage-clothing shops, kooky gift stores, artist studios, old-fashioned lolly shops and craft bookbinders. At night there are some cute little bars, and you might even see a penguin swaggering along the street – we did!

The precinct is at its liveliest on Sundays when the excellent Oamaru farmers market is in full swing. Note that some shops and attractions are closed on Mondays. There's also a brand new heritage center in the works; enquire about its progress at the i-SITE.

Nature's Wonders Naturally

Top choice wildlife reserve in Otago Peninsula

Price - adult/child $59/45

Hours - tours from 10.15am

Contact - http://www.natureswonders.co.nz; 03-478 1150

Location - Taiaroa Head, Otago Peninsula, New Zealand

What makes the improbably beautiful beaches of this coastal sheep farm different from other important wildlife habitats is that (apart from pest eradication and the like) they're left completely alone. Many of the multiple private beaches haven't suffered a human footprint in years. The result is that yellow-eyed penguins can often be spotted (through binoculars) at any time of the day, and NZ fur seals laze around rocky swimming holes, blissfully unfazed by tour groups passing by.

Depending on the time of year, you might also see whales and little penguin chicks.

The tour is conducted in 'go-anywhere' Argo vehicles by enthusiastic guides, at least some of whom double as true-blue Kiwi farmers. If you don't believe it, ask about the sheep-shed experience (price on application).

Te Papa

Museum in Wellington

Hours - 10am-6pm

Contact - http://www.tepapa.govt.nz; 04-381 7000

Location - 55 Cable St, Wellington, New Zealand

Te Papa is Wellington's 'must-see' attraction, for reasons well beyond the fact that it's New Zealand's national museum. It's highly interactive, fun, and full of surprises: aptly, 'Te Papa Tongarewa' loosely translates as 'treasure box'. The riches inside include an amazing collection of Māori artefacts and the museum's own colorful marae (meeting house); natural history and environment exhibitions; Pacific and NZ history galleries; the National Art Collection; and themed hands-on 'discovery centres' for children. Big-name temporary exhibitions incur an admission fee, although general admission is free.

You could spend a day exploring Te Papa's six floors and still not see it all. To cut to the chase, head to the information desk on level two and collect a map. For exhibition highlights and to get your bearings, the one-hour 'Introducing Te Papa' tour (adult/child $15/7) is a good idea; tours leave from the info desk at 10.15am, noon and 2pm daily. 'Māori Highlights' tours ($20/10) run at 2pm daily. Two cafes and two gift shops complete the Te Papa experience, which could well consume a couple of rainy-day visits. The museum's current star attraction is the state-of-the-art exhibition 'Gallipoli: The Scale of Our War', charting the country's involvement in WWI's Gallipoli campaign through the experiences of eight ordinary New Zealanders; key to the exhibition's impact are the hyper-real models produced by Weta Workshop, which bring it all to life. The museum will host the exhibition until 2018.

Waitangi Treaty Grounds

Historic site in Paihia & Waitangi

Price - adult/child $40/20

Hours - 9am-5pm Mar-24 Dec, 9am-6pm 26 Dec-Feb

Contact - http://www.waitangi.org.nz; 09-402 7437

Location - 1 Tau Henare Dr, Paihia & Waitangi, New Zealand

Occupying a headland draped in lawns and bush, this is NZ's most significant historic site. Here, on 6 February 1840, the first 43 Māori chiefs, after much discussion, signed the Treaty of Waitangi with the British Crown; eventually, over 500 chiefs would sign it. Admission incorporates entry to the Treaty Grounds, a guided tour and cultural

111

performance, and also entry to the new Museum of Waitangi. Admission for NZ residents is $20 upon presentation of a passport or driver's licence.

The importance of the treaty is well understood by a NZ audience, but visitors might find it surprising that there's not more information displayed here about the role it has played in the nation's history: the long litany of breaches by the Crown, the wars and land confiscations that followed, and the protest movement that led to the current process of redress for historic injustices.

The Treaty House was built in 1832 as the four-room home of British resident James Busby. It's now preserved as a memorial and museum containing displays, including a copy of the treaty. Just across the lawn, the magnificently detailed whare runanga (meeting house) was completed in 1940 to mark the centenary of the treaty. The fine carvings represent the major Māori tribes. Near the cove is the 35m waka taua (war canoe), also built for the centenary. A photographic exhibit details how it was fashioned from gigantic kauri logs.

Arthur's Pass National Park

National park in Arthur's Pass

Contact - http://www.doc.govt.nz

Location - Arthur's Pass, New Zealand

Straddling the Southern Alps and known to Māori as Ka Tiriti o Te Moana (steep peak of glistening white), this vast alpine wilderness became the South Island's first national park in 1923. Of its 1148 sq km, two-thirds lies on the Canterbury side of the main divide; the rest is in Westland. It is a rugged, mountainous area, cut by deep valleys, and ranging in altitude from 245m at the Taramakau River to 2408m at Mt Murchison. There are plenty of well-marked day walks, especially around Arthur's Pass village.

Pick up a copy of DOC's Discover Arthur's Pass booklet to read about popular walks including: Arthur's Pass Walkway, a reasonably easy track from the village to the Dobson Memorial at the summit of the pass (2½ hours return); the one-hour return walk to Devils Punchbowl falls; and the steep walk to beautiful views at Temple Basin (three hours return). More challenging, full-day options include Bealey Spur track and the classic summit hike to Avalanche Peak.

The park's many multiday trails are mostly valley routes with saddle climbs in between, such as Goat Pass and Cass-Lagoon Saddles Tracks, both two-day options. These and the park's longer tracks require previous tramping experience as flooding can make the rivers dangerous and the weather is extremely changeable. Always seek advice from DOC before setting out.

One Tree Hill

Top choice volcano in Auckland

Location - Auckland, New Zealand

This volcanic cone was the isthmus' key pa and the greatest fortress in the country. At the top (182m) there are 360-degree views and the grave of John Logan Campbell, who gifted the land to the city in 1901 and requested that a memorial be built to the Māori people on the summit. Nearby is the stump of the last 'one tree'. Allow time to explore surrounding Cornwall Park with its mature trees and historic Acacia Cottage (1841).

The Cornwall Park Information Centre has fascinating interactive displays illustrating what the pa would have looked like when 5000 people lived here. Near the excellent children's playground, the Stardome offers regular stargazing and planetarium shows that aren't dependent on Auckland's fickle weather (usually 7pm and 8pm Wednesday to Sunday, with extra shows on weekends).

To get to One Tree Hill from the the city take a train to Greenlane and walk 1km along Green Lane West. By car, take the Greenlane exit off the Southern Motorway and turn right into Green Lane West.

World of WearableArt & Classic Cars Museum

Top choice museum in Nelson

Price - adult/child $24/10

Hours - 10am-5pm

Contact - http://www.wowcars.co.nz; 03-547 4573

Location - 1 Cadillac Way, Nelson, New Zealand

Nelson is the birthplace of New Zealand's most inspiring fashion show, the annual World of WearableArt Awards Show. You can see 70 or so current and past entries in this museum's several sensory-overloading galleries, including a glow-in-the-dark room. Look out for the 'Bizarre Bras'.

More car than bra? Under the same roof are more than 100 mint-condition classic cars and motorbikes. Exhibits change, but may include a 1959 pink Cadillac, a yellow 1950 Bullet Nose Studebaker convertible and a BMW bubble car.

The World of WearableArt Awards Show began humbly in 1987 when Suzie Moncrieff held an off-beat event featuring art that could be worn and modelled. Folks quickly cottoned on to the show's creative (and competitive) possibilities. You name it, they've shown that a garment can be made from it; wood, metal, shells, cable ties, dried leaves, ping-pong balls... The festival now has a new home in Wellington.

Between the galleries, cafe and art shop, allow a couple of hours if you can.

Ulva Island

Top choice bird sanctuary in Stewart Island

Location - Stewart Island, New Zealand

A tiny paradise covering only 250 hectares, Ulva Island/Te Wharawhara is a great place to see lots of native NZ birds. Established as a bird sanctuary in 1922, it remains one of Stewart Island/Rakiura's wildest corners – 'a rare taste of how NZ once was and perhaps could be again', according to DOC. The island was declared rat-free in 1997 and three years later was chosen as the site to release endangered South Island saddlebacks.

Today the air is bristling with birdsong, which can be appreciated on walking tracks in the island's northwest as detailed in Ulva: Self-Guided Tour ($2), available from the Rakiura National Park Visitor Centre. Many paths intersect amid beautiful stands of rimu, miro, totara and rata.

Any water-taxi company will run you to the island from Golden Bay wharf, with scheduled services offered by Ulva Island Ferry. To get the most out of Ulva Island, go on a tour with Ulva's Guided Walks.

Goat Island Marine Reserve

Top choice wildlife reserve in Leigh

Contact - http://www.doc.govt.nz

Location - Goat Island Rd, Leigh, New Zealand

Only 3km from Leigh, this 547-hectare aquatic area was established in 1975 as the country's first marine reserve. In less than 40 years the sea has reverted to a giant aquarium, giving an impression of what the NZ coast must have been like before humans arrived. You only need step knee-deep into the water to see snapper (the big fish with blue dots and fins), blue maomao and stripy parore swimming around.

Excellent interpretive panels explain the area's Māori significance (it was the landing place of one of the ancestral canoes) and provide pictures of the species you're likely to encounter.

There are dive areas all around Goat Island, which sits just offshore, or you can snorkel or dive directly from the beach. Colourful sponges, forests of seaweed, boarfish, crayfish and stingrays are common sights, and if you're very lucky you may see orcas and bottle-nosed dolphins. Visibility is claimed to be at least 10m, 75% of the time.

Auckland Museum

Top choice museum in Auckland

Price - adult/child $25/10

Hours - 10am-5pm

Contact - http://www.aucklandmuseum.com; 09-309 0443

Location - Auckland Domain, Parnell, Auckland, New Zealand

This imposing neoclassical temple (1929), capped with an impressive copper-and-glass dome (2007), dominates the Auckland Domain and is a prominent part of the Auckland skyline, especially when viewed from the harbour. Admission packages can be purchased, which incorporate a highlights tour and a Māori cultural performance ($45 to $55).

The displays of Pacific Island and Māori artefacts on the museum's ground floor are essential viewing. Highlights include a 25m war canoe and an extant carved meeting house (remove your shoes before entering). There's also a fascinating display on Auckland's volcanic field, including an eruption simulation, and the upper floors showcase military displays, fulfilling the building's dual role as a war memorial. Auckland's main Anzac commemorations take place at dawn on 25 April at the cenotaph in the museum's forecourt.

Rotorua Museum

Top choice museum in Rotorua

Price - adult/child $20/8

Hours - 9am-5pm Mar-Nov, to 6pm Dec-Feb, tours hourly 10am-4pm, plus 5pm Dec-Feb

Contact - http://www.rotoruamuseum.co.nz; 07-350 1814

Location - Queens Dr, Government Gardens, Rotorua, New Zealand

This outstanding museum occupies a grand Tudor-style edifice. A 20-minute film on the history of Rotorua, including the Tarawera eruption, runs every 20 minutes from 9am. The Don Stafford Wing, dedicated to Rotorua's Te Arawa people, features woodcarving, flax weaving, jade and the stories of the revered WWII 28th Māori Battalion. Also here are two art galleries and a cool cafe with garden views (although the best view in town is from the viewing platform on the roof).

The museum was originally an elegant spa retreat called the Bath House (1908): displays in the former shower rooms give a fascinating insight into some of the eccentric therapies once administered here, including 'electric baths' and the Bergonie Chair.

Wairakei Terraces & Thermal Health Spa

Hot springs in Taupo

Price - thermal walk adult/child $18/9, pools $25, massage from $85

Hours - 8.30am-8.30pm Fri-Wed, to 7pm Thu

Contact - http://www.wairakeiterraces.co.nz; 07-378 0913

Location - Wairakei Rd

Mineral-laden waters from the Wairakei geothermal steamfield cascade over silica terraces into pools (open to those 14 years and older) nestled in native gardens. Take a therapeutic soak and a self-guided tour on the Terraces Walkway featuring a recreated Māori village, carvings depicting the history of NZ, Māori and local iwi (tribe) Ngāti

Tuwahretoa, and artificially made geysers and silica terraces echoing –
on a smaller scale – the famous Pink and White Terraces that were
destroyed by the Tarawera eruption in 1886.

The night-time Māori Cultural Experience (adult/child $104/52) – which
includes a traditional challenge, welcome, concert, tour and hangi meal –
gives an insight into Māori life in the geothermal areas.

Olveston

Top choice house in Dunedin

Price - adult/child $20/11

Hours - tours 9.30am, 10.45am, noon, 1.30pm, 2.45pm & 4pm

Contact - http://www.olveston.co.nz; 03-477 3320

Location - 42 Royal Tce, Dunedin, New Zealand

Although it's a youngster by European standards, this spectacular 1906 mansion provides a wonderful window into Dunedin's past. Entry is via fascinating guided tours; it pays to book ahead. There's also a pretty little garden to explore.

Until 1966 Olveston was the family home of the wealthy Theomin family, notable patrons of the arts who were heavily involved with endowing the Public Art Gallery. This artistic bent is evident in Olveston's grand interiors, which include works by Charles Goldie and Frances Hodgkins (a family friend). A particular passion was Japanese art, and the home is liberally peppered with exquisite examples. The family was Jewish, and the grand dining table is set up as if for Shabbat dinner.

Mt Eden

Top choice volcano in Auckland

Location - 250 Mt Eden Rd, Auckland, New Zealand

From the top of Auckland's highest volcanic cone (196m) the entire isthmus and both harbours are laid bare. The symmetrical crater (50m deep) is known as Te Ipu Kai a Mataaho (the Food Bowl of Mataaho, the god of things hidden in the ground) and is considered highly tapu (sacred). Do not enter it, but feel free to explore the remainder of the mountain. The remains of pa terraces and food storage pits are clearly visible.

Until recently it was possible to drive right up to the summit but concerns over erosion have led to restricted vehicle access. Paths lead up the mountain from six different directions and the walk only takes around 10 minutes, depending on your fitness.

Botanic Gardens

Top choice gardens in Christchurch

Hours - 7am-8.30pm Oct-Mar, to 6.30pm Apr-Sep

Contact - http://www.ccc.govt.nz

Location - Rolleston Ave, Christchurch, New Zealand

Strolling through these blissful 30 riverside hectares of arboreal and floral splendour is a consummate Christchurch experience. Gorgeous at any time of the year, the gardens are particularly impressive in spring when the rhododendrons, azaleas and daffodil woodland are in riotous bloom. There are thematic gardens to explore, lawns to sprawl on, and a playground adjacent to the Botanic Gardens Information Centre.

Guided walks ($10) depart at 1.30pm (mid-September to mid-May) from the Canterbury Museum, or you can chug around the gardens on the Caterpillar train.

Cape Reinga

Landmark in Cape Reinga & Ninety Mile Beach

Standing at windswept Cape Reinga Lighthouse (a rolling 1km walk from the car park) and looking out over the ocean engenders a real end-of-the-world feeling. This is where the waters of the Tasman Sea and Pacific Ocean meet, breaking together into waves up to 10m high in stormy weather. Little tufts of cloud often cling to the ridges, giving sudden spooky chills even on hot days.

Visible on a promontory slightly to the east is a spiritually significant 800-year-old pohutukawa tree; souls are believed to slide down its roots. Out of respect to the most sacred site in Māoridom, don't go near the tree and refrain from eating or drinking anywhere in the area.

Zealandia

Wildlife reserve in Wellington

Price - adult/child/family exhibition only $9/5/21, exhibition & admission $18.50/10/46

Hours - 9am-5pm, last entry 4pm

Contact - http://www.visitzealandia.com; 04 920 9213

Location - 53 Waiapu Rd, Wellington, New Zealand

This groundbreaking eco-sanctuary is hidden in the hills about 2km west of town: the Karori bus (No 3) passes nearby, or see the Zealandia website for info on the free shuttle. Living wild within the fenced valley are more than 30 native bird species, including rare takahe, saddleback, hihi and kaka, as well as tuatara and little spotted kiwi. An excellent exhibition relays NZ's natural history and world-renowned conservation story.

More than 30km of tracks can be explored independently, or on regular guided tours. The night tour provides an opportunity to spot nocturnal creatures including kiwi, frogs and glowworms (adult/child $75/36). Cafe and shop on-site.

Huka Falls

Top choice waterfall in Taupo

Location - Huka Falls Rd, Taupo, New Zealand

Clearly signposted and with a car park and kiosk, these falls mark where NZ's longest river, the Waikato, is slammed into a narrow chasm, making a dramatic 10m drop into a surging pool. From the footbridge you can see the full force of this torrent that the Māori called Hukanui (Great Body of Spray). Take one of the short walks around the area, or walk the Huka Falls Walkway back to town or the Aratiatia Rapids Walking/Cycling Track to the rapids.

On sunny days the water is crystal clear and you can take great photographs from the lookout on the other side of the footbridge.

Museum of Waitangi

Top choice museum in Paihia & Waitangi

Price - adult/child $40/20

Hours - 9am-5pm Mar-24 Dec, 9am-6pm 26 Dec-Feb

Contact - http://www.waitangi.org.nz; 09-402 7437

Location - 1 Tau Henare Dr, Paihia & Waitangi, New Zealand

The new Museum of Waitangi is a modern and comprehensive showcase of the role of the Treaty of Waitangi in the past, present and future of New Zealand. The second storey is comprised of the Ko Waitangi Tēnei (This is Waitangi) exhibition and the ground floor features special temporary exhibitions and an education centre. Many taonga (treasures) associated with Waitangi were previously scattered around NZ, and this excellent museum is now a safe haven for a number of key historical items.

Admission incorporates entry to the Waitangi Treaty Grounds, a guided tour and a cultural performance.

Taupo Museum

Top choice museum in Taupo

Price - adult/child $5/free

Hours - 10am-4.30pm

Contact - http://www.taupodc.govt.nz; 07-376 0414

Location - Story Pl, Taupo, New Zealand

With an excellent Māori gallery and quirky displays, which include a
1960s caravan set up as if the occupants have just popped down to the
lake, this little museum makes an interesting rainy-day diversion. The
centrepiece is an elaborately carved Māori meeting house, Te Aroha o
Rongoheikume. Historical displays cover local industries, a mock-up of
a 19th-century shop and a moa skeleton, and there's also a gallery

devoted to local and visiting exhibitions. Don't miss the rose garden alongside.

Set up in a courtyard, the 'Ora Garden of Wellbeing' is a recreation of NZ's gold-medal-winning entry into the 2004 Chelsea Flower Show.

Whangarei Art Museum

Top choice gallery in Whangarei

Price - admission by donation

Hours - 10am-4pm

Contact - http://www.whangareiartmuseum.co.nz; 09-430 4240

Location - The Hub, Town Basin, Whangarei, New Zealand

At the Te Manawa Hub information centre, Whangarei's public gallery has an interesting permanent collection, the star of which is a 1904 Māori portrait by Goldie. Also planned is the Hundertwasser Arts Centre, based on architectural plans by the late Austrian artist Friedensreich Hundertwasser. See www.yeswhangarei.co.nz for details of the campaign to raise support and funding for the project. A model of the proposed design can be seen at Hundertwasser HQ, a pop-up store designed to increase awareness of the project.

Te Mata Peak

Park in Hastings & Around

Contact - http://www.tematapark.co.nz; 06-873 0080

Location - off Te Mata Rd, Hastings & Around, New Zealand

Rising melodramatically from the Heretaunga Plains 16km south of Havelock North, Te Mata Peak (399m) is part of the 1-sq-km Te Mata Trust Park. The summit road passes sheep trails, rickety fences and vertigo-inducing stone escarpments, cowled in a bleak, lunar-meets-Scottish-Highlands atmosphere. On a clear day, views from the lookout fall away to Hawke Bay, Mahia Peninsula and distant Mt Ruapehu.

The park's 30km of trails offer walks ranging from 30 minutes to two hours: pick up the Te Mata Park's Top 5 Walking Tracks brochure from local i-SITEs.

Wallace Arts Centre

Top choice gallery in Auckland

Hours - 10am-3pm Tue-Fri, to 5pm Sat & Sun

Contact - http://www.tsbbankwallaceartscentre.org.nz; 09-639 2010

Location - Pah Homestead, 72 Hillsborough Rd, Hillsborough, Auckland, New Zealand

Housed in a gorgeous 1879 mansion with views to One Tree Hill and the Manukau Harbour, the Wallace Arts Centre is endowed with contemporary New Zealand art from an extensive private collection, which is changed every four to six weeks. Have lunch on the veranda and wander among the magnificent trees in the surrounding park. The art is also very accessible, ranging from a life-size skeletal rugby ruck to a vibrant Ziggy Stardust painted on glass.

Bus 299 (Lynfield) departs every 15 minutes from Queen St (outside the Civic Theatre) and heads to Hillsborough Rd ($5, 40 minutes).

Conclusion

Thank you for reading this book, if you found it useful please consider some of my other books at www.amazon.com/author/alexpitt.

Made in the USA
Lexington, KY
26 February 2018